first names

EARHART

Andrew Prentice

Illustrations by Mike Smith

For Lottie

First Names: AMELIA EARHART
is a
DAVID FICKLING BOOK

First published in Great Britain in 2019 by
David Fickling Books,
31 Beaumont Street,
Oxford, OX1 2NP

Text © Andrew Prentice, 2019
Illustrations © Mike Smith, 2019

978-1-78845-023-2

1 3 5 7 9 10 8 6 4 2

Mixed Sources
Product group from well-managed
forests and other controlled sources
www.fsc.org Cert no. TT-COC-2139
© 1996 Forest Stewardship Council
FSC

DAVID FICKLING BOOKS Reg. No. 8340307

A CIP catalogue record for this book is available from the British Library.

Printed and bound in Great Britain by Clays Ltd, Elcograf S.p.A

The facts in *First Names: Amelia Earhart* have been carefully checked
and are accurate to the best of our knowledge, but if you spot something
you think may be incorrect please let us know.
Some of the passages in this book are actual quotes from Amelia and other
important people. You'll be able to tell which ones they are by the style of
type: *I did not kill a cow on landing – unless one died of fright.*

Who will you get to know next?

Watch out for
Malala Yousafzai and Ada Lovelace

CONTENTS

Introduction – Kansas, Winter 1907

It hadn't been this cold since eighteen-hundred-and-froze-to-death, but that didn't stop Amelia. She crouched over her sled and went through her pre-jump routine. Check the runners were free of ice. Check the snow was good. Check there weren't no lollygagging slowpokes clogging up her run.

Check. Check. Check.

'Tally-hoooo!' Amelia jumped, landed hard on her belly and shot down the hill like a comet.

When it snowed – and in Kansas, snow meant deep, glorious, school-obliterating blizzards – all the children in town knew there was only one place to be. The hill that ran from the top of North Second Street was perfect for sledding.

Traditionally, only the boys 'belly-slammed'. This meant they rode down the hill on their stomachs, head first. All the girls sat upright for a more ladylike trip.

Except for Amelia. She **loved speed more than anything** and didn't care a fig for what anyone thought. Amelia had always been different – and she **never got scared**.

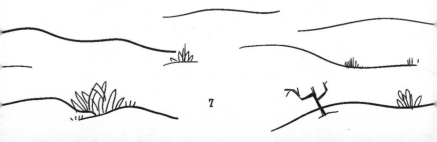

A cart pootled out into the middle of the road. The hill was so icy that Amelia couldn't turn or stop. And she was going much too fast anyway. The horse had enormous blinkers, so it couldn't see her coming. The driver couldn't hear everyone's screams of warning. Amelia had about **three seconds to save her own life**. Plunging towards certain death, Amelia didn't blink. Instead she went faster, steering with her toes as she aimed for the only gap she could see.

Whoosh! Her sled zipped between the front and back legs of the horse so fast that the driver didn't even notice.

Soon, plenty of people *would* take notice of Amelia Earhart. In fact within thirty years she'd become the **most famous woman in the world**. She was bigger than the biggest movie stars. Hotter than the sun itself.

Amelia, you see, moved on from sleds to planes. She became a pilot – and back then, in the great golden age of flying, pilots were top of the tops. They soared across the heavens like heroes from legends. Adventure, danger and death were never far away.

Amelia became the most famous pilot of them all. She broke records, crossed oceans and achieved things that no one – man or woman – had ever achieved before.

She stayed different – and she never got scared.

Wait a minute, that's not exactly true!

Well, that's how it seemed to everyone who knew you.

9

I got the collywobbles same as anyone, while I was getting ready. But they stopped as soon as I was up in the air. When you're flying, you're far too busy to be frightened.

So you worried when you were packing your suitcase?

Every time.

But when your instruments gave out, your engine was on fire, your plane was iced up and you started tumbling towards the hungry waves . . . **you weren't scared at all** then?

Not really. Thing is, when you're plummeting towards certain doom, you don't feel scared. You just 'do'. If you do right, you stay alive. And if you don't, well . . .

But why did you put yourself in all that danger, Amelia?

Well, if you'll just get on with my story you'll find out soon enough.

1   AMELIA ARRIVES

Amelia Mary Earhart zipped into the world on 24th July 1897. Her parents, Amy and Edwin Earhart, were delighted with their cheerful, fat little baby. They wrapped her up in white starched dresses and nicknamed her Millie. A couple of years later they gave her a sister, Muriel. No one ever called her Muriel, though. The youngest Earhart was soon much better known as Pidge.

Millie's early years in Kansas and Iowa were happy ones. Her dad, Edwin, had a good job as a lawyer for the railways, though **he dreamed of bigger things**. In his spare time he tried to come up with an invention that would make his family's fortune. He squandered hundreds of dollars to make a new signal flag for trains, but sadly his flag never fluttered. As hard as Edwin tried, he never really got anywhere, which must have been frustrating.

There were some advantages to having a father who was a bit out of the ordinary. Take Christmas for instance. Millie never wanted the girly presents she was expected to ask for. She wasn't interested in dolls, or pretty dresses; instead **she went for baseballs and fishing rods and sleds**. And her father gave them to her. He believed a girl should have what she wanted, no matter what anyone else said. And one Christmas, Millie received a very unusual present.

It was a 0.22 calibre Hamilton rifle, to go with the packet of bullets she'd found in her stocking!

Not everyone was happy. Millie's grandparents were rich and grand and they'd never approved of Edwin and his strange ways (they thought their daughter was too good for him). **Grandma almost fainted** with surprise.

Millie and Pidge had cleaned out the barn by Boxing Day.

Millie's dad wasn't just generous at Christmas. **He took his family on amazing adventures** as well.

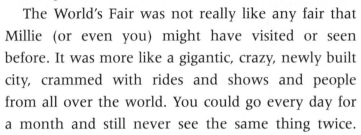

The World's Fair was not really like any fair that Millie (or even you) might have visited or seen before. It was more like a gigantic, crazy, newly built city, crammed with rides and shows and people from all over the world. You could go every day for a month and still never see the same thing twice.

You could visit the actual cabin where Abraham Lincoln was born, have your photo taken with Geronimo, the famous Apache war chief, or watch a real sea battle fought on the lake. You could ride double-dipping log chutes, visit a fake cloud that was someone's idea of what Heaven is actually like and swoop about on **the greatest merry-go-round ever built**.

wow!

Even the food was mind-blowing. Some say the hot dog bun, the cheeseburger and the ice-cream cone were all invented at the fair.

When Millie came back home she was so excited about the rides that she made her uncle help her **build a rollercoaster** in their back yard.

Millie was always good at planning, but even more importantly for someone with big dreams,

she didn't just have ideas, she finished them off too. Her rollercoaster was greased with lard and in their test runs without a rider it ran pretty fast.

Amelia insisted on being the first person to try it. She climbed up high, sat herself inside the crate, took a deep breath and plunged.

It worked even better than she'd hoped. When she reached that little dip at the bottom, she didn't just coast to a stop, **she actually took off**, zooming through the air!

She came to rest metres away, covered in dust, cackling with laughter.

'Oh, Pidge!' Millie said. 'It's just like flying. I'm going again.'

This was too much for Millie's mum, who insisted that they take the coaster apart at once.

Dad's Sickness

In a way, that famous trip to the fair was too much for Edwin too. To fund the holiday, he'd squandered money they didn't have – just another bad decision in the series of bad decisions that he'd made and would keep on making. Soon, despite a promising career and a happy family, **Edwin started drinking** heavily.

Of course no one realized he had a problem, at first. To the children he was still their dad, as jolly and generous as ever. But the boozing was getting worse. He started making mistakes at work and drinking in bars all afternoon. He broke promises and lied. He quarrelled with his wife.

Edwin's life spiralled quickly out of control and soon he was fired from his job. Millie and Pidge went away with their mum while he tried to sort himself out, but the family ran out of money and one winter **they couldn't even pay for firewood**.

'Dad's sickness' was awful for the girls. Not just because they lost their father, but because they'd lost their way of life too. Back then, the American Midwest was ruled by a strict moral code. You did the right thing. You went to church. You kept your head down and worked hard. You got married, and had children. You certainly didn't lose all your money and have a drunk for a father.

The Earharts were shamed and shunned. Suddenly Millie was an outcast. **She lost all her friends**. The family moved to a different town and her father disgraced himself again, so she lost her new friends too. Fed up, Amy sent Edwin away again, and they moved to another house. Amelia ended up changing schools four times as a teenager.

This hardened me up, I can tell you. I wouldn't wish it on anyone.

Those years must have been very tough. But, funnily enough, Millie didn't react to her troubles the way you might think. Instead of trying to fit in and be like all the other girls in the new towns she moved to, she stubbornly insisted on doing things her own way.

Not Fair For Girls

Millie must have stuck out like a sore thumb. The other girls all wore skirts, but **Millie wore trousers** whenever she could – they felt more comfortable. She tried to play basketball with the boys. She complained that her teachers weren't teaching her properly. People always noticed how different she was, but she didn't care. Look at her high-school yearbook:

Most likely to bake a cake

Future bank manager

The girl in brown who walks alone

The thing was, Millie was always different.

19

2   Amelia Gets A Chance

Amelia turned eighteen in 1915. She'd nearly grown up – she didn't call herself Millie any more – and she had big dreams. She didn't want to just get married and have children, like most girls of the time. She wanted something else, though she wasn't quite sure what it was. But with no money and a disgraced family it was hard to see how she'd ever escape to a better world.

Then, out of the blue, **everything changed**. Amelia's upright, uptight granny died, and Amy Earhart inherited a bit of money. Suddenly she could afford to send Amelia and Muriel to a finishing school that would prepare them for college.

> We needed a bit of a polish so we could pass our exams!

Amelia was over the moon – suddenly **a bigger and better world had opened up** for her just like that.

Even at her posh new school in Philadelphia, Amelia didn't change her ways, and by the end of her first year she'd managed to turn the place upside down. One story says she got the school's sorority system – a nasty, back-stabbing popularity contest –

banned. She campaigned to have modern subjects like science taught to the girls. She played the ukulele at midnight feasts. She was elected class vice-president.

Keep the noise down – I've got exams tomorrow!

After years of struggle Amelia was flourishing; so it was a bit of a shock to everyone when she didn't finish her second year at the school.

Amelia's sister Muriel (hardly anyone called her Pidge these days) was at a different school, in Toronto, and during the Christmas holidays Amelia went to visit her. In Toronto train station, she was horrified when she noticed **four one-legged soldiers** helping each other down the platform. As soon as she left the station she saw there were many more terribly wounded soldiers – it was the first real evidence she'd seen of the First World War that was still raging in 1917. The soldiers' pain and sacrifice shocked Amelia and stirred something inside her.

Back at school her easy life seemed like a sideshow. Amelia knew **she had to do something**, anything, to help those soldiers. Before long she'd quit school for ever.

> I was nineteen and a grown woman. No one could stop me!

She dashed off a quick letter to her mother and jumped on the next train back to Canada. In Toronto she joined the VAD (Volunteer Aid Detachment) as a nurse and began caring for wounded and shell-shocked soldiers at the Spadina Military Hospital.

Amelia grew up fast. She worked long hours, six days a week. She scrubbed floors, ladled out medicine from a bucket and played tennis with the soldiers. On her days off she went riding with her sister. Both the Earhart girls were brilliant with horses.

At the stables one horse caught Amelia's eye: a notoriously bad-tempered stallion named Dynamite that no one had been able to ride.

The groom warned her that Dynamite had thrown two soldiers the day before. But **Amelia never backed down from a challenge**. She began stopping by the stable every evening to bring Dynamite an apple. Within a month she'd tamed the savage beast and was riding him around the yard.

Amelia became famous among the soldiers after that – she was the only one who managed to stay on Dynamite's back.

A few of the soldiers were so impressed that they invited her to a flying show. This was to be her first close encounter with an aeroplane. It was a bitterly cold winter's day, and Amelia was standing so close to the plane that **snow whipped up by the propellers stung her in the face**. The propellers stirred up something else inside her too, a little seed of excitement.

I'll make them scatter!

Amelia was rooted to the spot.

That little red airplane whispered something to me as it swished by.

Strangely enough, even when the war ended in 1918, the danger didn't stop. Suddenly everyone was threatened by a different enemy, one that was even worse. As the soldiers returned from the fighting, a terrible plague swept across the world. The Spanish flu was frighteningly deadly and killed fast. A healthy adult man could wake up quite cheerfully, brush his teeth with pep and vigour, have a good, hearty breakfast and still be dead by sundown. A fifth of the world went down with the flu. **Fifty million people died**.

Amelia worked harder than ever as the flu burned like wildfire through the hospital. Exhausted, it wasn't exactly surprising that she caught the bug herself; for two months **she fought for her life**, coughing and choking as her lungs filled with infected fluid. But she recovered, thank goodness. She was one of the lucky ones.

Another Fresh Start

After her brush with death, Amelia resolved to concentrate on living. She was 22 now and, inspired by her work in the hospital, she enrolled on the pre-medical course at Columbia University in New York – the first step on the path to becoming a doctor.

This was a brave and unusual thing for a girl to do.

At that time only a few women were even in training to be doctors, let alone working in hospitals. Amelia quickly settled down to her studies and did well, but she hadn't lost her love of adventure. She discovered a **network of secret tunnels** beneath the university and persuaded her friend Louise to help her explore every nook and cranny. The pair also monkeyed about on the rooftops at night. Once they even managed to get all the way to the top of the dome of the university library.

But just like before, after less than a year of study, Amelia was forced to leave her new school. This time it was her folks that needed help. Amelia's mum and dad were giving their marriage one last crack. Edwin was making a fresh start in California – he swore he'd given up the booze for good – and Amy had agreed to go out there and live with him. They both wrote letters to Amelia pleading with her to come and help keep the peace.

No doubt if she'd been a boy they wouldn't have thought to ask – but Amelia was a loyal daughter, even if she wasn't a conventional one. In spite of all the important things she longed to do, she found it impossible to turn her parents down.

'I'll see what I can do to keep Mother and Father together, Pidge,' she told her sister as she boarded the California train. 'But after that I'm coming back here to live my own life.'

As it turned out, she wouldn't be back for five whole years.

Amelia might have walked away from her dreams, but she needn't have worried. As she steamed towards Los Angeles, her true destiny was getting closer and closer. Almost from the first moment she set foot in the city, **her life was blown onto a completely new path**.

Edwin still loved to treat his daughter, even when she was 23, and it was the barnstorming air show he took Amelia to that started *everything* . . .

Amelia Explains: Barnstorming

When the First World War ended, America was flooded with brave pilots and cheap planes.

Daredevil stuntmen and women began to tour the country in aerial circuses. They flew between small towns, as the wind and their whim took them, and soon they became known as 'barnstormers'.

Wow! He certainly stormed that barn!

Holy Cow!

They'd borrow a field from a farmer for the day, then advertise their arrival by flying several low passes right down the main street – roaring over shops and schools as low as they could, spooking cows, blasting hats from old ladies' heads and putting a broad grin on the face of every child in town.

The town shut down for an immediate holiday. Everyone flocked to the field and bought tickets for the show. The bravest would buy plane rides too.

I wanna go in one of those!

Like everyone else, Amelia was totally gobsmacked by the acrobatic daring of the pilots, the speed of the planes and the howling scream of the engines. She stared in wonder at the sky and immediately resolved that she had to get up there herself – **she wanted to become an `aviatrix`**.

On the way home she quietly asked her dad to find out how much it would cost to have flying lessons. Going along with Amelia's 'little joke', Edwin made some enquiries. He soon found out that the price was $1,000 (about £10,000 today).

This was a lot of money, even for a man as generous as Edwin. But Amelia hadn't changed. She still wanted to do stuff that only boys were meant to do, and her father still found it impossible to turn her down. It only cost $10 for a ten-minute ride with one of the barnstormers, so Edwin paid up and off Amelia went. Poor old Edwin didn't know what he was letting himself in for.

I'm sure he thought that one ride would be enough for me.

Amelia flew with one of the pilots she'd watched the day before, a man with a perfect pilot's name: Frank Hawks. They looped out over Los Angeles and the blue Pacific Ocean. It was a clear winter's day. The waves rolled in far below. The sun glinted on rooftops and tiny palm trees and yellow beaches. Amelia could see for miles . . .

They touched down in a cloud of dust. **Amelia didn't want to leave her seat**.

3   AMELIA TAKES TO THE SKY

Nowadays, as we zoom round the world in air-conditioned steel tubes, chomping peanuts and zoning out on bad movies, we hardly know that we are flying at all. When Amelia first went up, flying was more dangerous and much newer than space flight is to you.

Borrrrr-ing!

There were accidents all the time. Sooner or later, most of the early pioneering aviators died in crashes. And even though flying got a little bit safer in the 1920s, it was still terrifyingly risky. As late as 1927, airmail pilots, who worked for a flying postal service, had a **life expectancy of only 900 hours** in the air. That's about six months if you fly an average of five hours a day, every day. Only the brave and the foolhardy ventured into the sky.

So Amelia's new passion for flying was a big deal. Imagine asking your parents to spend a fortune so you could go swimming in volcanoes, or jump off a mountain wearing one of those terrifying flying-squirrel suits. Would they pay up?

Amelia didn't care. The flying bug had sunk its teeth into her. She was certain – even though she knew it was horribly dangerous – that the only thing she could do in life now was fly a plane.

Her dad didn't agree without a fight. First, he argued that he didn't have the money. So Amelia went out and got a job as a typist, vowing to pay him back. Then he said that she could have lessons, but he didn't like the idea of her spending time alone with a man in the cockpit, so **she'd have to be taught by a woman**.

Daddy thought he had me licked, but he didn't stand a chance.

Amelia had already found a female instructor: Neta Snook. As well as having an amazing name, Neta was a pioneering female pilot. She'd recently barnstormed across America in a plane she'd rebuilt herself, and now she'd come to Los Angeles to do stunt work and aerial advertising.

LEARN TO FLY!

Edwin finally admitted defeat. The next morning Amelia pulled on a pair of high-laced boots and squeezed into her riding breeches. Then, with the wind singing in her blood, she headed off to a dusty Californian airfield to capture her dream.

The dawn of flight was a mad, crazy time.

In the space of about twenty years at the beginning of the twentieth century, humanity raced into the sky. In less than a generation, we went from flying only in our dreams, to taking off in real rickety, fragile death traps, and then – without pausing for breath – we were suddenly swooping about the sky like we'd always belonged there.

Wright Flyer, 1903

Wilbur and Orville Wright made the world's first flight at Kitty Hawk in North Carolina. Pretty amazing for a pair of brothers who started out running a bicycle shop.

Their flight lasted just 12 seconds and they travelled a full 120 feet (36 metres)!

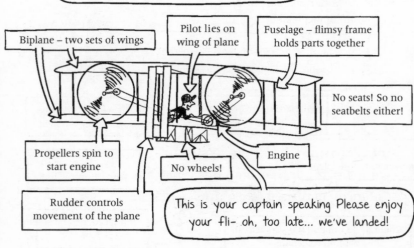

Biplane – two sets of wings

Pilot lies on wing of plane

Fuselage – flimsy frame holds parts together

No seats! So no seatbelts either!

Propellers spin to start engine

No wheels!

Engine

Rudder controls movement of the plane

This is your captain speaking Please enjoy your fli- .oh, too late... we've landed!

Bleriot XI, 1909

Six years later, Frenchman Louis Bleriot proved that planes weren't just toys for rich kids; they could actually change the world.

Which way to Dover, mademoiselle?

Monoplane – one set of wings

Rudder

Propeller spins to start the engine

Top speed: 47 mph (76 km/h)

Wheels

Bleriot was the first person to fly across the English Channel (22 miles) – in just 36 minutes! He went on to design many more planes.

Fokker Dr.I, 1917

New planes were developed for the First World War, and fighter aces fought duels in the sky. A German pilot nicknamed the Red Baron flew a Fokker Dr.I.

He shot down more than 80 planes before he finally lost a fight.

Ailerons – moving parts on wing help steer plane

Triplane – has three sets of wings; strong but light

Rudder controls movement of the plane

Wings staggered so pilot can see better

Could fly 185 miles (300 kilometres) without refuelling

Top speed: 115 mph (185 km/h)

The Jenny, JN-4

The Jenny was America's most important First World War biplane.
Nine out of ten US pilots trained in one of these.

Up, Up and Away!

It was barely a week since her first flight. But Amelia was in a hurry. She'd gone **absolutely flying-doollally**, and now she was about to have her first lesson.

To Amelia's frustration, Neta took things slowly. The first sessions were spent learning how to taxi the plane on the ground and use the controls. In fact the first two weeks were all based on the ground. Neta did fly Amelia up a few times, but Amelia was never actually in control of the plane.

At last the day finally came: Amelia was to take the stick on her own.

Her heart was hammering in her chest as she climbed up onto the fuselage, crawled forward and lowered herself carefully into the cramped front cockpit. Suddenly it was actually happening.

They were flying a rickety Canuck – a type of Jenny. Amelia had to be careful because if she stepped in the wrong place **her foot could go right through the wing** – the plane was that fragile.

The cockpit was completely open. There was no safety belt. Above Amelia sat the broad sweep of the upper wing. That looked sturdy at least.

A dusty man spun the propeller and the engine rattled into life. Everything was shaking and bouncing about, including Amelia's thoughts.

There were so many things she might forget!

'Remember!' Neta shouted. 'The biggest rule is don't go too slow! You don't want to stall. **Keep the speed up**!'

Because of the pounding blood in her head, and the roar of the engine, Amelia could barely hear her, even though Neta's cockpit was just behind hers.

'And if you make a mistake, I might not be able to save us!' shouted Neta. 'So make sure you don't!'

Amelia tried to forget that. She put her hand on the stick. She felt the vibrations running through her body. It was as if the Jenny was alive and eager to go.

'Ready?' shouted Neta.

'Ready!' Amelia answered. She waved her hand. Then the little plane was bumping over the grass, picking up speed. The wind whipped past, tugging at Amelia's flying cap. She felt every bump in the field. She felt the plane dip to the side and pulled hard on the stick. It was heavy, but it moved. They were straight again.

The plane surged forward. Another huge rattling bump, and another, and then, all of a sudden, they weren't bumping any more. They were rising smoothly.

Amelia pulled the stick back. The ground fell away. She soared up and up.

'Feel that, Amelia?' Neta screamed. 'You're flying!'

'I am!'

And for the first time in her life, **Amelia Earhart felt free**.

4   AMELIA EARNS HER WINGS

Amelia was obsessed. She would be a pilot or die trying. It was easy to see why her parents were worried.

In order to pay for lessons, she'd now got a new job at the telephone exchange. Amelia's mum hated this, but she couldn't complain to her daughter, because Amelia was never home. When she wasn't working or sleeping, she spent every spare second at the tiny, dusty airport known as Kinner Field.

Even though her parents were unhappy, Amelia was blooming. The Kinner crew were a close-knit band of adventurers. Every one of them was **bonkers about flying** and there were always jobs to do around the airfield. Wings needed patching. Wooden struts snapped and needed replacing. Engines had minds of their own. Amelia wasn't shy about getting her hands dirty, and she was quickly accepted by the gang of pilots and mechanics.

She also became great friends with Neta Snook, and even adopted Neta's style: leather jacket, trousers and a flying cap. This was obviously quite practical, given all the greasy machines she fiddled with, though the other pilots teased Amelia when she bought her first flying jacket. It was much too shiny and new. Amelia solved the problem by not taking it off for a week, and rubbing it with engine oil. She even slept in it. Soon it was battered and creased just like everyone else's.

The last stage of her transformation started when she was walking down the long road to the airfield. A little girl and her father picked her up in their car.

'What do you do?' asked the little girl, looking Amelia up and down.

'I am learning to be a pilot,' replied Amelia.

'But you don't look like an aviatrix,' said the girl, with a frown. '**You have long hair**!'

That night, Amelia started cutting her hair in secret. So as not to horrify her mother, she only cut off a little bit at a time – maybe half an inch a week – and kept her hair up when she was at home. After a few months her long mane was gone. Now she wore a short, tousled bob. She never changed her hairstyle after that.

Despite these outward changes, Amelia took her time when it actually came to flying. She had more lessons from Neta, and from an ex-army pilot named John Montijo, who taught her stunts: dives, tailspins, loops and barrel rolls.

Tailspin   Barrell roll   Dive

If the plane was upside down and spinning like a top, I wanted to know how to recover. But it was glorious fun too.

She also **had her eyes on a new purchase**. Bert Kinner, the owner of the airfield, was a designer of planes, and the prototype of his first model, the Kinner Airster, was just being finished as Amelia started her lessons.

The Canary-Yellow Plane

This Airster was bright yellow, very fast and handled like a kite (once it got off the ground – take-offs and landings were a bit tricky). Better still, because it was so much lighter than some of the older machines, Amelia could lift up its tail and turn the plane round herself without needing to ask for help. If she ever had enough money to buy one – and pay for the fuel – this little beauty would offer her the freedom she craved.

Amelia soon decided that her life would be incomplete without the Airster. There was just one problem: **no one thought she should buy it** – and Neta was dead against it. Unlike the Jenny, the Airster was not a beginner's plane. It might be quick and nimble, but it was as light as a leaf, its engine was prone to choking and it had a tendency to flip on its head on landing, squashing the plane and the pilot flat!

Then there was the price. An Airster cost $2,000 (about £19,250 today). Yet another vast pile of money to add to the huge sums that Amelia was already paying out for lessons and fuel. However, she would not be beaten. Although her father refused to pay a cent, she scraped together all her savings, persuaded her mother and sister to chip in as well and worked out a deal with Bert.

In July 1921, Amelia got her first plane at last, but a few days later **she had her first crash**! Just after take-off, the Airster's engine choked with oil (as it did quite often) and began sputtering. Amelia, with Neta in the back seat as a passenger, was faced with a nasty choice: go into a dive and risk smashing into a grove of eucalyptus trees, or try to pull the plane up and smash a little slower into the same clump of trees.

She pulled up.

The Kinner ploughed into the branches. The propeller and the landing gear were crushed. Amelia bit her tongue badly, but otherwise she was absolutely fine. When Neta got out of the plane, she found her student calmly powdering her nose.

Amelia, what are you doing?

I just want to look myself when the reporters come.

It was the first crash of many – but in those days being lucky was part of being a good pilot. Crashes were a rite of passage, and over the next few months Amelia had several more: she ran out of fuel and landed in a cabbage patch; a few weeks later she landed in mud so deep the wheels got stuck. The most dangerous smash came when they landed the Airster on an un-mown runway. Choked with weeds, the plane came to a sudden halt, tipped forward and **threw Amelia out of the cockpit**.

But now came Amelia's biggest test, because Neta and John Montijo finally judged her ready for her first solo flight. For any pilot this is a terrifying moment. All your training boils down to a single question: **can you actually fly**?

Amelia charged down the runway in her Airster. The engine rattled so fiercely she couldn't feel her legs on the rudder pedals. As she tried to take off, one of the shock absorbers snapped, causing a wing to sag. Amelia screeched to a halt, narrowly avoiding disaster.

Any normal person would have waited for another day, but not Amelia. After some quick on-the-spot repairs she set off again. This time she soared into the air. Again, most people on their first solo flight are happy with a couple of steady loops around the airfield and an easy landing. But not Amelia. Thoroughly unconcerned by her recent brush with death, she flew up to 5,000 feet (1,500 metres) and **started doing aerobatics**. Down on the ground, Neta and John could hardly bear to watch, but Amelia brought the canary-yellow Airster home safely.

Flying High

Amelia could fly, but it was proving harder than ever to find the money to pay for fuel. Petrol was much more expensive in those days than it is now. So Amelia worked harder; she'd take whatever job she could find to earn money for the fuel she needed to fly. By her own account she had **28 different jobs** over the next few years: she drove a gravel truck, sold sausages and even persuaded her family to invest in a gypsum mine. She worked in a photographic studio too, and began taking a camera with her everywhere she went.

When she could afford to go up in the air, Amelia was already showing what she could do. One day she gave her dad and sister the shock of their lives...

Amelia soared all the way up to 14,000 feet (4,250 metres), **smashing the women's altitude record**. Funnily enough, her record probably only lasted a couple of weeks – another pioneering female pilot would soon have climbed even higher. That was the way it went with the early fliers: they were constantly trying to push further and fly faster and higher.

The competition was as fierce as it was dangerous. On Amelia's next attempt a few months later, she flew into thick cloud at 10,000 feet (3,000 metres). In an open cockpit that can be deadly. There was no escaping the cold, moist fog. The world turned white and some of the instruments went on the blink, as sleet and snow iced up the plane.

Now Amelia had no idea where she was or how high. Even worse, the engine had started sputtering. A spark plug had given out. Keeping cool, Amelia put the plane into a spin, whirling down to escape the cloud. **Each tumbling second felt like an eternity**, but at last she glimpsed a patch of clear sky and the ground. She landed safely, but the record remained unbroken.

Amelia's achievements were now being noticed. In 1923 she was awarded her pilot's licence by the Fédération Aéronautique Internationale. She was only the sixteenth woman in the world to earn the honour. Now all the records she had broken were official, but sadly **not everyone was happy for her**. After an article about Amelia appeared in the *New York Times*, one of her relatives wrote her an extraordinary letter, which said: *'The only time a lady's name should appear in print is at her birth, her marriage and her funeral.'*

See how we women were treated? That old uncle must have whirled in his grave with what came later!

Disaster!

Remember the gypsum mine Amelia had invested in to help pay for her flying? Things weren't going well. Peter Barnes, her friend who ran the mine, got in touch to say one of the trucks they were using had been hit by a train. A new one would cost $7,000. Amelia was **forced to sell** her beloved Airster to help buy the replacement. But worse was to come. Production had fallen way behind, so Edwin and Amelia went out to the desert near Las Vegas to help.

While they broke their backs shovelling gypsum into canvas bags, a torrential downpour started. A flash flood rushed down the ravine, washing away its banks. The mine was about to be swept away! Amelia, Edwin and two of the miners escaped in one of the trucks, barely making it across a bridge over the ravine. When Peter tried to drive across after them, **the bridge's struts gave way**. The whole thing collapsed and the second truck dropped into the raging torrent. Peter was drowned.

Amelia had narrowly escaped with her life. She'd lost a good friend, the mine was destroyed and all the family money was gone. To cap it all, her parents' marriage was over for good. Edwin asked Amy for a divorce. Amy was devastated and Amelia was disgusted, because her father was drinking again.

The Canary-Yellow Sports Car

While she'd had a plane, the plan had been to fly across the country. Now there was little to keep Amelia in California, so, with the last of her money (and ignoring some overdue bills), she bought a bright yellow sports car she nicknamed the 'Yellow Peril'. **If she couldn't fly, she would drive all the way** to Boston. She set off in spring 1924 with her mum.

Even driving back then was a bold adventure. There were few highways and most roads were little more than dirt tracks. What's more, the Earharts took the scenic route. First they visited the huge trees in Sequoia National Park, then Yosemite and Crater Lake. All this time they were heading north. When they drove right on into Canada, Amy started to worry that Amelia would never turn east.

Wherever they stopped, crowds gathered. Cross-country driving – especially in a canary-yellow car **driven by a woman** – was still a novelty. Dusty backwoods towns came to a stop when Amelia rolled in. For Amelia, the trip must have felt like **earthbound barnstorming.**

Chatting with the friendly crowds, it would have been on this trip too that Amelia got her first taste of celebrity. It would come in useful later on.

As the crow flies, Los Angeles is about 3,000 miles (4,828 kilometres) from Boston. Amelia and her mother went on a 7,000-mile (11,265-kilometre) wander instead. They finally arrived in Boston with the car covered in stickers from all the places they had visited.

For now the adventures had to stop. Amelia had been suffering from a sinus infection for some time and needed several painful operations. The treatment was expensive and again Amelia was left with little money for flying. After trying out a few jobs, she settled on being a social worker, teaching English at Denison House, a settlement home for newly arrived immigrant families that helped them find their feet in their new country.

Amelia was still mad about planes though. She wrote passionate letters to the newspapers promoting the training of female pilots. She joined a flying club and managed to go up a few times a month. She kept her dreams of adventure alive. This was important – no matter how unlikely it seemed – because **Amelia's luck was about to change**.

In April 1928 Amelia Earhart was rehearsing a play with her students at Denison House. A phone call came for her, and at first she refused to take it – no one came between Amelia and her students. But the caller was so insistent, she finally gave in. **Amelia was absolutely furious** as she picked up the reciever – she no idea her whole life was about to be flipped upside down.

RING!　　RING!

5　　AMELIA TAKES THE PLUNGE

The future was arriving faster than you could think. It was thrilling and astonishing. Pilots and their planes were the biggest news around. Each new, daring feat made headlines around the world.

Plane mania had reached a climax in May 1927 when Charles Lindbergh became the first person to fly solo across the Atlantic Ocean. **The entire world went bananas**.

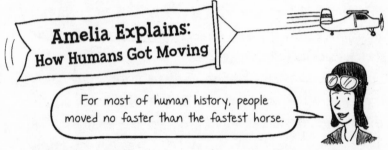

Amelia Explains:
How Humans Got Moving

For most of human history, people moved no faster than the fastest horse.

✈ In the Age of Exploration (which really got going with Christopher Columbus in 1492), we discovered that the world was round and that, if we had a couple of years to spare, we could sail all the way around it. Horses were still as fast it got.

Hey! Isn't this where we started from?

✈ In the Age of Steam (1820s onwards), ships could move much faster and then railways shrank the world. By the end of the nineteenth century we could travel fairly quickly from one end of a country to another. But we were still travelling on the ground, on rails, to someone else's timetable. And it still took weeks to cross an ocean.

Wait!

Don't worry. There'll be another along next week.

Then, in the 1880s, cars were invented. Imagine yourself the proud owner of one of these new-fangled machines. You didn't need to take a train. You could drive where you liked, and you'd get there a little bit faster than you would on a horse. That's certainly progress.

Wait! What's that strange thing in the sky? Is that . . . Is that a flying machine?

For all of humanity's existence we'd slogged along at ground level. Now, suddenly, all the ways we had of measuring space and time and distance were BLOWN APART.

Charles Lindbergh

Charles Lindbergh flew across the Atlantic from New York to Paris in 33.5 hours, without a navigator or companion, completely on his own.

A crowd of 150,000 people were waiting for his plane, the *Spirit of St. Louis*, to land. They dragged him from the cockpit and carried him around the field on their shoulders.

Charles had started out as a barnstorming pilot, trained with the US Army flying school, and then flown the airmail postal service from St. Louis to Chicago.

But after this flight, he was suddenly the most famous man in the world.

The Big Question

When Amelia picked up the phone in April 1928, the deep voice at the other end of the line belonged to a journalist and 'fixer' named Hilton Railey. He had **one very serious question** for Amelia:

Do you want to become the first woman to fly across the Atlantic?

Yes, of course!

Deadly Flights

In 1927 alone, apart from Charles Lindbergh's successful flight, 14 people died trying to cross the Atlantic by air. The huge distance and unpredictable weather pushed the planes of the day to their limit.

✈ Before 1928 no woman had made the crossing, as pilot or passenger, though five had tried – and failed – and three had died!

✈ Elsie Mackay, early pilot, movie star and daughter of an earl, had set off from Britain with her one-eyed, fighter-ace co-pilot Walter Hinchliffe, in March 1928. They were never seen again.

✈ Ruth Elder flew east from New York, with her instructor George Haldeman. They got within 360 miles (580 kilometres) of Spain before they were forced down into the sea. The plane blew up in the water, but luckily Ruth and George were rescued.

Amelia didn't seem at all put off by the threat of danger. In fact it really excited her. She wasn't put off by fame either. Just being brave enough to attempt the crossing – as passenger or pilot – would guarantee any woman **worldwide celebrity**. In fact, the race to be that first woman had just about reached boiling point. Two challengers were already vying with each other, both desperate to win the title.

Deadly Rivals

Amy Guest

Fabulously wealthy
American heiress. Aged 55.

Amy was a mother of three, a
feminist and promoted votes for
women. She was also keen on
hunting, and rode side saddle
over huge fences.

Mabel Boll

Glamorous American adventuress.
Aged about 30.

Mabel pretended she was an
heiress, but was actually a bartender's
daughter. She was nicknamed
`The Queen of Diamonds´ and
was famous for her fiery temper.

In March 1928 – just as news of Elsie Mackay's
disappearance hit the headlines – Mabel Boll
dramatically announced her intention to become the
first woman to cross the Atlantic in a plane.

Amy Guest was determined to beat her. She hated the idea of the publicity-hungry Diamond Queen becoming the most famous woman in the world.

Amy didn't tell her family, but – in a stunning piece of skulduggery – she bought not just Mabel's plane, but her pilot and co-pilot out from under her feet!

Fokker F.VII called *Friendship*.

Mabel quickly found a new ride and a new crew, and **the race was on**.

Then, at the last minute, Amy's son discovered what she was plotting. He threatened to abandon his university exams and lock up his mum in her mansion to stop her from going!

Wright-Bellanca WB–2, known as *Miss Columbia*.

It's your own fault, Mother.
BANG!
BANG!

Amy had to back out reluctantly, but she was still **stubbornly determined** to defeat Mabel Boll. And if she couldn't do it herself, she'd just have to find the right woman to do it for her. Which is why Amelia got the phone call in the first place.

Amy had a 'shopping list' for the kind of woman she wanted:

1. A modern American woman ✔

2. The right kind of good looking ✔

3. Intelligent, well-spoken and from a good family ✔

4. Very brave because she'd be risking her life ✔

5. Helpful if she can fly a plane – though she won't get her hands on the equipment, she'll only be a passenger ✔

Whatever you think about Amy's snobbish list, there is no doubt that Amelia Earhart **ticked all the boxes**. So Hilton Railey invited her to New York to be interviewed at once. Amy Guest spared no expense. She'd asked the publisher George Putnam, who had been the mastermind behind Lindbergh's flight, to organize everything. He would also have exclusive rights to publish the story.

They left me in the corridor kicking my heels for an hour! I went in angry! But they still picked me.

Shh! It's A Secret

George Putnam was very impressed with Amelia's quiet courage and air of cool competence. Two days later, Amelia signed a contract to fly across the Atlantic. They weren't offering to pay her a cent, but she didn't care. One of the things Amelia liked about the project was that **this was a woman's flight**: paid for and organized by a woman to show just what her sex was capable of doing. In any case, George explained, she could make pots of money giving talks about her experience, if they succeeded.

She borrowed a heavy wool flying suit from a friend, without telling him what she was using it for. In fact, **she was sworn to secrecy** and hadn't told a soul what she was planning. Her mum, dad and sister had no idea what Amelia was up to until after she had left Boston for Newfoundland.

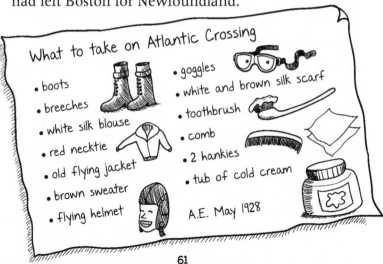

What to take on Atlantic Crossing

- boots
- breeches
- white silk blouse
- red necktie
- old flying jacket
- brown sweater
- flying helmet

- goggles
- white and brown silk scarf
- toothbrush
- comb
- 2 hankies
- tub of cold cream

A.E. May 1928

The plan was to fly Amy's plane, the *Friendship*, to Newfoundland – the closest point to Europe in North America – and attempt the crossing from there. The plane was to be piloted by Wilmer Stultz, better known as Bill, and his mechanic Louis Gordon. Amelia hoped to take the stick as well, if conditions allowed.

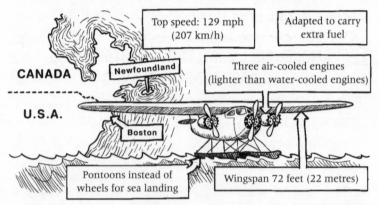

Top speed: 129 mph (207 km/h)

Adapted to carry extra fuel

CANADA Newfoundland

Three air-cooled engines (lighter than water-cooled engines)

U.S.A.

Boston

Pontoons instead of wheels for sea landing

Wingspan 72 feet (22 metres)

They were meant to fly for Newfoundland immediately, but bad weather and poor visibility kept the *Friendship* grounded for several weeks. When the weather was fine in Boston it was foggy in Newfoundland, and vice versa. To pass the time **Amelia drew up a will**, and sent letters to her family to be opened if she didn't make it back.

Here's what she actually wrote to her dad:

Dearest Dad

Hooray for the last grand adventure! I wish I had won but it was worthwhile anyway. You know that.

I have no faith that we'll meet anywhere again, but I wish we might.

Anyway, goodbye, and good luck to you.

Affectionately, your doter
Mill

On 3rd June the weather turned at last and the *Friendship* flew off. The news broke at once:

BOSTON GIRL STARTS FOR ATLANTIC HOP

There was huge interest around the world – interest that was stoked by Mabel Boll's announcement that she too was about to set off:

MABEL BOLL CHALLENGES BOSTON RIVAL TO RACE ACROSS ATLANTIC

Amelia's family were mobbed by reporters eager for news of America's newest heroine. A crowd of journalists camped outside their doors and followed them wherever they went. They also **made up stories**, because neither parent would tell them anything.

> She's doing it to pay off your debts, isn't she?

> How dare you!

Meanwhile, the *Friendship* had landed in Trepassey Harbour in Newfoundland. Large crowds came out to see Amelia and her crewmates, but for the next week they were all frustrated. The weather turned again and they were trapped in the harbour by gales and fog. Even when the weather was fine, the narrow harbour made take-off difficult if the wind or the tide were in the wrong direction.

Again and again they tried to take off – but the plane waddled across the water and failed to lift. On 12th June, Amelia wrote in her log:

This has been the worst day . . . the sea so heavy that the spray was thrown so high that it drowned the motors. We unloaded every ounce of stuff from the plane – camera, my coat, bags, cushions – we would have made it but for the (wet) motors... We are all too disappointed to talk.

With a break in the weather, Mabel Boll got the chance she'd been waiting for and made the flight to Newfoundland. Her pilot was a First World War flying ace, and her plane, *Miss Columbia*, was much faster than the *Friendship*. It used runways for take-off, too, while the *Friendship* was a seaplane, and **struggled to take off** when the sea was rough. Mabel landed and was given a celebratory banquet by the mayor. Amelia was not invited.

Stuck!

Each day the *Friendship* had failed to take off in Trepassey, the crowd that had come to watch dwindled. Bill Stultz was one of the best pilots in the world, but he was getting frustrated. **He started drinking** – putting the flight and their lives at risk!

The weather turned worse, and Mabel Boll taunted the crew of the *Friendship* with a telegram suggesting they make a race of it. While Mabel drank champagne in her hotel, Amelia and her crew struggled to get their plane out of the water.

The *Friendship* was carrying a huge weight of fuel – enough to make it across the Atlantic – but each time they failed to take off, they siphoned a little more away to lighten the load. They'd started out with 870 US gallons (3,293 litres), but soon this was cut to 830 then 800. Even so they couldn't make it into the air. Bill Stultz drank more as the pressure mounted.

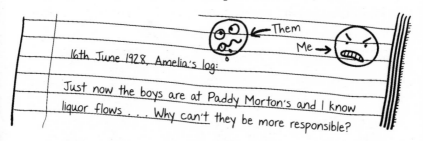

← Them
Me →

16th June 1928, Amelia's log:

Just now the boys are at Paddy Morton's and I know liquor flows . . . Why can't they be more responsible?

While the boys were out, a telegram arrived. The weather forecast predicted a short window in the storms over the Atlantic. This might be their last chance.

The next day, Bill was horribly hungover and **refused to fly**, saying it was too risky. But Amelia wouldn't back down. She and Louis Gordon splashed cold water on the pilot's face and fuelled him up with gallons of coffee. Then they dragged him, still protesting, to the plane.

Bill was just about ready to go, but now the *Friendship* did not co-operate. By 11.30 that morning they had already made two failed attempts at take-off. The plane was still too heavy to get out of the water. With every failure, Amelia became more worried that Mabel Boll was getting the jump on them. Desperate, the crew were forced to make an awful sacrifice. They pumped 100 US gallons (378 litres) of fuel out of the tank. With only 700 US gallons (2,646 litres) left, they were **flying at the absolute limit of their range** – they couldn't afford to make a single mistake.

Bill gave it one last try. To Amelia it felt like the most dangerous hour of her life. The *Friendship* bounced across the choppy seas, soaking two of the three engines in saltwater.

Amelia crouched in the cabin with a stopwatch in her hand to check the take-off time, and with her eyes fixed on the air-speed indicator. She knew that if it passed 50 mph (80 km/h), the *Friendship* would fly.

Thirty miles per hour, forty – the *Friendship* was slowing down again.

After a long pause, the indicator climbed to fifty.

Fifty…fifty-five, then sixty mph. **They were off at last**!

Only a few people were watching. The crowd had lost hope that the plane would ever take off.

Mabel Boll chose not to fly that morning. She'd seen the weather reports and decided it wasn't worth the risk. She waited with the rest of the world.

In fact, Mabel Boll never made the trip.

Over The Atlantic

The clear weather didn't last for long. About 300 miles (480 kilometres) out of Trepassey, the *Friendship* was buried in thick cloud. Amelia shivered and shook as the plane rumbled through the sky. She wore earplugs to avoid being deafened. Searching for clear air, Bill Stultz flew up into a snowstorm. With no de-icing equipment, he was forced to dive quickly below it. Amelia was **thrown across the cabin**, sliding into the oil drums. Bill's stamina was fading – struggling to stay awake, he handed the controls over to Louis Gordon and fell asleep in the co-pilot's chair.

This was **the biggest storm** Amelia had ever flown through. Worse, the cloud made it hard to know their position, and they really couldn't afford to lose their way. Fortunately, after eight hours, they managed to make contact with a British ship and get their bearings. The ship promised to radio New York, where soon headlines blared:

As the fuel load lessened, the plane was able to fly higher. At last the *Friendship* could climb to 10,000 feet (3,000 metres) and out of the thick, turbulent cloud. It was much colder in the high, clear air, and the three aviators donned their fur-lined flying suits. The North Star appeared over the wing. Taking it in turns to sleep, they watched the eastern horizon for the long-awaited glow of dawn and munched egg sandwiches. Unluckily for Amelia, Bill didn't trust her to take control of the plane. He hardly let Louis touch the stick either.

They had been flying for about sixteen hours when Bill took the plane down below the clouds to see where they were. They reckoned they only had **two hours of fuel left**. With the coming of the dawn light they hoped they'd be able to spot Ireland below them. Instead they found only open ocean.

They were lost.

19th June 1928, Amelia's log:
Everything shut out. 5000 feet now. Awfully wet. Water dripping in windows. Port motor coughing. Sounds as if all the motors are cutting.

The *Friendship* was in a very tight spot. They couldn't find Ireland! Louis Gordon called vainly over the radio for ships to 'come in', but none did. The radio was broken, they were running out of fuel and **the engines were starting to misbehave**.

Suddenly they spotted a few ships in the sea below – but they were sailing diagonally across the *Friendship's* path when they should have been sailing parallel. The *Friendship* was **flying in the wrong direction**! Desperate, the crew wasted more precious fuel trying to communicate with one of the boats.

Amelia scribbled a note asking for their location and wrapped it tightly around an orange. But when they tried to bomb the ship with it, she missed – twice.

So they gave up and rattled on, desperate to find land.

The fog sank lower. Now they were flying just 500 feet (152 metres) above the waves. If something went wrong there was no room for manoeuvre. There was **less than an hour's worth of fuel** left in the tank.

The next 30 minutes were agony until, at last, they glimpsed a small fleet of fishing boats beetling across the water. Slowly, wonderfully, a dark blue shadow emerged out of the mist.

'Land!' screamed Louis, and in his excitement he threw his egg sandwich out of the open window.

The *Friendship* touched down at 12.40 p.m. on 18th June. They had been flying for 20 hours and 40 minutes. With no idea where they were, they tied up to a buoy floating at the mouth of a river. The green, wet dampness of the British countryside had never looked so inviting.

Amelia Earhart sank back in her nook as the engines stuttered to a halt. After twenty long hours in the plane there was a brief moment of quiet . . . but it wasn't going to last for long.

6   AMELIA FINDS FAME

They'd done it! Amelia had become the first woman to cross the Atlantic, and Louis Gordon and Bill Stultz had made sure it happened. But there was no fanfare and no welcoming committee – which was hardly surprising, seeing as **no one was expecting them**!

The locals weren't in any great hurry to greet the mystery aviators either. Three men were working on a railway track by the shore. The crew climbed onto the plane's float and waved and shouted, but after briefly glancing up the men went back to work.

It took half an hour for a fisherman to row out to the plane.

As it turned out, the *Friendship* had landed in Burry Port in south Wales – over 100 miles (160 kilometres) from Ireland, where they thought they were!

The Welsh welcome started out low-key, but news of their safe arrival on the other side of the Atlantic soon spread. Telegrams zipped around the world. Hilton Railey, who had been waiting in Southampton, where the *Friendship* had intended to land, raced up by seaplane to meet them. This was **the biggest news story in the world**, and he wanted

to make damn sure no one else got to it before him. Other journalists came speeding in by car and plane and train. All of a sudden this little port in Wales was the most important spot on the planet.

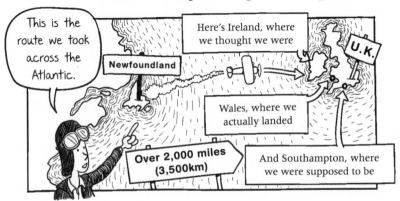

Hilton arrived in less than three hours, but a jubilant crowd of 2,000 people had already gathered on the shore by then. When he rowed out to Amelia, however, he was surprised. She seemed downcast – not just tired, but depressed.

'Aren't you thrilled?' Hilton asked. 'This is incredible! You did it!'

'No,' said Amelia. 'I was just baggage, like **a sack of potatoes**. Maybe someday I'll try it alone.'

Needless to say Hilton didn't let *that* quote get out – he wanted to keep his heroine heroic; that way they'd sell more papers.

At last Amelia and the pilots were taken ashore. The first thing they wanted was a hot bath – but before that they had to face the jubilant crowd. Only a few hours before they'd all been terrified out of their wits, convinced they were about to crash into the sea and drown. Now **Amelia was worried she would be ripped to pieces** by the mob. Well-wishers desperate for souvenirs tore at her clothes and stole her scarf. She even had to be rescued by the police.

The world's press were no better. They were eager for news, and to Amelia's intense embarrassment she was all they cared about. While Bill and Louis were completely ignored, no tiny detail about her life was too small.

Amelia did her best to give credit to the pilots, but no one was interested – it was her story they wanted to hear. Giant banner headlines all over the world were screaming her name. Amelia was the heroine and there was nothing she could do about it.

One Big Party

Travelling on to London, Amelia was celebrated everywhere she went. She was invited to the most exclusive parties and the grandest houses. She hobnobbed with dukes and debutantes, and a flock of reporters breathlessly recorded her every breath. Bill and Louis went completely unnoticed. Meanwhile, **Hilton Railey had to hire four secretaries** to deal with the mountain of letters that were piling up in Amelia's hotel room.

Amelia was having the time of her life. Think of the contrast: one minute you're teaching English to immigrant families in a dingy classroom, the next you're plunged into a whirlwind of dances, galas and receptions. You have long queues of famous and fabulous people desperate to meet you, and a cheering throng applauds you everywhere you go. At least to begin with, **the madness must have been exhilarating**. But then...

Amelia Earhart blew her nose!

GASP!

AMAZING!

PARP!

Amelia quickly understood that in just one flight she had become far more than plain old Amelia Earhart. Now, like it or not, she stood as a shining symbol of what it was possible for a woman to achieve. Important people wanted to listen to what she had to say. And so, in speech after speech, she told them what she thought. It wasn't always what they wanted to hear.

If the pioneer has good ideas nobody will ask whether the pioneer is man or woman. And here is where Atlantic flights by women, or any other good flight helps – it starts other women to think.

What utter tosh!

Amelia Earhart was getting a lot of women thinking.

The Heroine Returns

When she sailed back to America, **32 cities** asked to put on a parade just for her. Amelia picked three: New York, Boston and Chicago. In each city she and her co-pilots were roared through the streets as bands blared and ticker tape rained down from the sky.

Nice turnout!

She was America's darling. And George Putnam, the man who'd masterminded the Atlantic crossing, wanted to keep her that way. He knew the fame game better than anyone and explained to Amelia the great opportunity that lay at her fingertips: money, celebrity and influence were hers for the taking – but only if she kept working harder than ever.

The trouble was, the 'great American public' had the attention span of a forgetful goldfish. Newspapers were always quick to move on to the next big thing. So if Amelia wanted to buy the gas to fuel her dreams, she'd have to keep doing things to get herself noticed.

Amelia had always been hardworking, and now **she worked like a maniac**. Staying in George's house, she wrote her autobiography and the account of her famous flight in just a few weeks. And with George's publicity machine to drive it, her book – *20 Hours 40 Minutes: Our Flight in the Friendship* – became an instant bestseller.

George And His Publicity Machine

✘ George Putnam had already discovered that adventure was a gold mine. He and his friends went on expeditions, sold their stories to newspapers and then wrote books that sold like hotcakes. It was a good way to make a lot of money.

Hold it right there, Mr Putnam.

✘ In 1926, after Putnam and his pals had sailed to the Arctic, George's battle with a giant walrus made front-page news. His three accounts of the trip were all bestsellers – published by G. P. Putnam's Sons, George's famiy's publishing company!

> ✈ George realized before most that celebrity was powerful and profitable. A huge audience existed now, bigger than ever before, and they were desperate to be entertained.
>
> ✈ The press could make you a star, but they could break you just as easily. Over the next few years, Putnam worked tirelessly to protect Amelia and support her career. He also made sure that Amelia kept her nose to the grindstone. Staying famous was hard work.

Adventures In The Air

The day after Amelia finished writing, she started planning a transcontinental flight – the reverse of the trip that she'd wanted to make four years earlier. She would be the first woman to fly solo across America from the Atlantic to the Pacific. She had a new plane and more than enough money for fuel – the advances from books and speaking tours had given her the freedom to fly that she'd always craved, but the press were still caught up in an 'Amelia frenzy' and followed her every move.

George, who was of course masterminding all the publicity, flew with her for the first leg of the journey. But the first story to come out of the trip was a bad one. On the opening flight, **Amelia made a botched landing** and the plane swung round, smashing its left wing, undercarriage and propeller. Needless to say, the press went to town:

EARHART CRASHES

DISASTER IN PITTSBURGH

WOMAN PILOTS A DANGER

Amelia still had a long way to go to convince people that women could make good pilots. George pulled himself from the wreckage and went straight to work on the story. His press statements after Amelia's crashes (and there would be many of these in the future) were always the same. It was a mechanical breakdown or a bumpy runway that was to blame. It was never Amelia's fault.

This was far from the truth – especially in the early days of Amelia's flying career. Although she had learned to fly fairly competently, **she wasn't the expert aviatrix that George told everyone she was**. The new planes that she was flying now were much more powerful and harder to handle than the ones that she'd trained in.

All the same, once her plane was fixed, the flight west was great fun. Like the barnstormers before her, Amelia took off each morning from a small town and landed a few hours later in a field, a street or – if she was lucky – a tiny, unmarked airfield. She was finally having the adventures she'd dreamed about as a girl. All the newspapers tracked her progress, but they couldn't keep up with her plane.

The wind and sun burned her face brown except for the patch where her goggles sat around her eyes. When she checked herself in the mirror she said **she looked like a horned toad**.

Amelia reached California in August and went to visit her father. While she was there, she was invited to be a guest of honour at that year's National Air Races in Los Angeles. She couldn't compete though – women weren't allowed to! In any case, she didn't stay for long – Amelia needed to make the return flight to New York so that she could become the first woman to fly from the Atlantic to the Pacific and back again.

Air Races

In the 1920s and 1930s, air racing was a thrilling new sport and Americans flocked to see it! Every year hundreds of thousands of spectators crammed into the National Air Races, the biggest contest of them all. Events included cross-country point-to-point races that took place over many days and covered thousands of miles.

Then there was pylon racing, where several pilots took off at the same time and raced each other around a circuit, with the route marked out by pylons 50 feet (15 metres) high. The courses were usually 10 miles (16 kilometres) long.

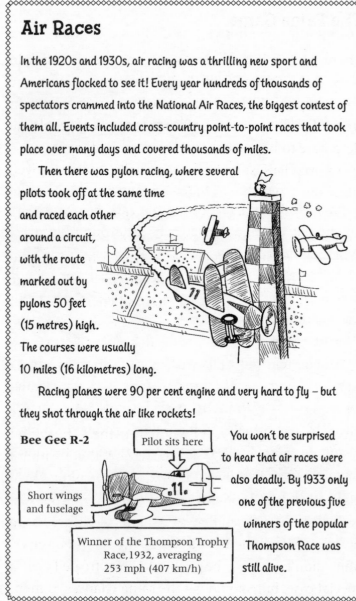

Racing planes were 90 per cent engine and very hard to fly – but they shot through the air like rockets!

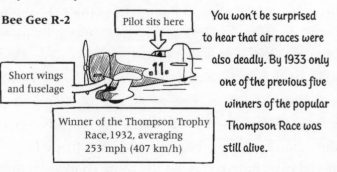

Bee Gee R-2

Pilot sits here

Short wings and fuselage

Winner of the Thompson Trophy Race, 1932, averaging 253 mph (407 km/h)

You won't be surprised to hear that air races were also deadly. By 1933 only one of the previous five winners of the popular Thompson Race was still alive.

The Fame Game

There was no letting up. As soon as she was back in New York, George had Amelia buzzing around the country on a lecture tour. She had to stand up in front of huge audiences, **often thousands of people**, all desperate to hear what their heroine had to say.

To Amelia's surprise she actually quite enjoyed these talks, which was lucky because she'd give quite a few of them over the years. Her speech was usually much the same. She'd always start with a joke to get the crowd on her side, and show she wasn't stuck up. Then she'd move on to her main theme: the awesome wonder of flight and how in the future everyone would be zooming around the world by plane. (She wasn't far wrong there either.) Sprinkled throughout she'd also offer her thoughts about more controversial issues: she urged women to explore new careers, to become independent and stand up for themselves. She didn't think they should be treated as a special case, but should get the same chances as men.

Optimists and pessimists were important in the invention of flying. The optimists invented the airplane and the pessimists the parachute.

These tours were only half the work. To keep Amelia's name in the papers, George helped her plan and fund a constant stream of airborne adventures. Flying was expensive, so Amelia needed more money than ever.

Her problem was that aeroplane technology was moving forward at breakneck speed. A plane that was cutting edge on the day you bought it could be way out of date just six months later. By 1929 the Avro Avian that Amelia had bought after her Atlantic flight the previous year was slow and unreliable compared to the planes her rivals were flying. That was a disaster, because Amelia was keen to fly in a race that was being planned for the summer. And **she wanted to win**.

The Powder Puff Derby

The National Air Races had finally planned a cross-country race from Los Angeles to Cleveland that was only open to women. Every famous female pilot had signed up. As soon as the Women's Air Derby was announced, one journalist jokingly called it the 'Powder Puff Derby' and, whatever the women thought of it, the name stuck.

Amelia pumped her contacts and scraped together enough cash to buy a Lockheed Vega 5B – a big monoplane, much faster and trickier than anything she'd flown before. She called it her:

'Little Red Bus'

Lockheed Vega 5B

One-piece wing

Light and strong monocoque fuselage (wooden shell moulded into shape; no support struts inside)

Top speed: 165 mph (265.5km/h)

Cabin for carrying up to four passengers

The cockpit was high off the ground and your legs rested practically under the engine mount, making the heat build-up pretty uncomfortable at times… Fast, unstable, tricky near the ground with a monocoque fuselage that would collapse like a packet of cornflakes in a crash.

Elinor Smith, pilot.

The race had nine stages over nine days. **It was a fearsome test of endurance and skill** for the pilots, who had to get up at four in the morning and hardly got a chance to rest during the day.

And they're off...

DAY 1

Twenty pilots enter the race, but one doesn't make it to the start . . .

DAY 2

Mary Haizlip's plane is damaged. She arrives late and should be disqualified, but the other pilots are good sports and agree she can fly.

Marvel Crosson is forced to bail out, but her parachute fails to open and she dies!

Wait for me!

There goes my chance of getting my name in a book.

Sabotage! Claire Fahy finds wires under her wing have been snapped.

YIKES!

DAY 3

DAILY NEWS

SHAMBLES! WOMEN CAN'T FLY OR RACE

DAY 4

Amelia is winning, but crashes in Yuma – overturns and hits a cactus.

Not again!

Amelia came third in the Derby. She was disappointed, it wasn't the win she'd hoped for, but it was a still a triumph. Elinor Smith, who was by no means a fan of Amelia's, witnessed her exhausted landing in Cleveland, where the Vega bounced inelegantly to a stop:

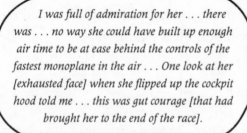

I was full of admiration for her . . . there was . . . no way she could have built up enough air time to be at ease behind the controls of the fastest monoplane in the air . . . One look at her [exhausted face] when she flipped up the cockpit hood told me . . . this was gut courage [that had brought her to the end of the race].

Amelia was still not quite the pilot George's publicity machine would have everyone believe. But she was getting better – and anything she lacked in skill she more than made up for in pluck.

Afraid? No, I wish I'd been. I didn't think of it. Fear is more or less an emotional attitude.

Nineteen racers had started the race and, **incredibly, sixteen had finished** – a much higher proportion than in similar men's races of the time. The women had flown their dangerous planes across the country with nothing more than road maps and compasses to guide them. It was a fantastic achievement.

Making the most of all the publicity after the race, Amelia and the other women pilots set up a new organization called the Ninety-Nines to support women who loved to fly and keep track of their achievements. Amelia became its first president. The club is still going strong today and it's still the leading organization for women fliers in America.

Soaring Higher

Over the next few years, Amelia continued to keep herself in the public eye. In 1930 she set the women's air-speed record. She set two more women's records over the next ten days. A year later she flew an experimental plane called an autogyro – an early helicopter – from coast to coast and back again. It was hard to fly and **she crashed several times**, but Amelia was the first woman pilot of the autogyro, and she set an unofficial altitude record of 19,000 feet (5,790 m).

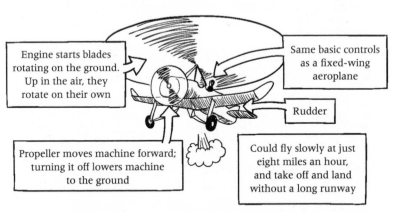

Engine starts blades rotating on the ground. Up in the air, they rotate on their own

Same basic controls as a fixed-wing aeroplane

Rudder

Propeller moves machine forward; turning it off lowers machine to the ground

Could fly slowly at just eight miles an hour, and take off and land without a long runway

Amelia had her fingers in so many pies it was hard to keep track of them all. Everyone wanted a piece of her. She'd been working for *Cosmopolitan* magazine since 1928, writing articles with titles such as 'Shall You Let Your Daughter Fly?' and 'Why Are Women Afraid to Fly?' She'd been asked by the government to advise them on flying regulations. She even found time to set up her own airline (although it later went bankrupt), as well as keeping up her frantic schedule of speaking engagements. Amelia always had something going on.

But despite all this excitement, the newspapers were in a frenzy about Amelia's private life. Rumours had been flying around for months. In December 1929, George Putnam's wife had sued him for divorce. In those days, **a divorce was scandalous** enough, but George and Amelia had been spending an awful lot of time together, and they hadn't just been working hard: **they'd fallen in love**! Over the next few months George asked Amelia to marry him five times. And five times she refused.

In any case, Amelia had something else on her mind. Her father was seriously ill. She often flew out to California to see him, but in September 1930, a few hours after she had left his bedside, he died peacefully in his sleep.

On her way back east after his funeral, miserable with grief, Amelia had **the worst accident of her career** so far. As she came in to land in Norfolk Virginia, her plane went nose over tail and she was very nearly scalped!

Amelia Says 'Yes'

Perhaps because of her father's death, or perhaps because of George's incredible persistence, in late 1930 Amelia finally accepted his sixth marriage proposal. There was going to be no big celebrity wedding, though. As a result of the scandal they got married in secret **without any guests at all**! Amelia hadn't even told her family.

The thing was, Amelia was intensely worried about this huge step. She was afraid she would lose the independence and freedom that she had worked so hard for. Just before the wedding ceremony, she gave George a handwritten letter. It said quite plainly what a **terrible idea** she thought their marriage was and asked him to promise never to interfere in her work or her play.

George was so **utterly smitten** with her that he readily agreed.

Amelia was more fun to play with than anyone else – I admired her ability, stood in awe of her intelligence, adored her imagination, and loved her for herself.

In those days not many husbands would have accepted Amelia's terms, but George's big promise was about to face a big test.

Ever since the Atlantic crossing, some unfinished business had been gnawing at Amelia. She was famous for being little more than a 'sack of potatoes'. Now she was determined to put that right.

7   AMELIA GOES SOLO

At breakfast one morning in 1932, Amelia looked up from her plate of bacon and eggs and said quietly, 'George, would you mind if I flew the Atlantic?'

To his credit, George didn't spit out his coffee, or choke on his yolk. He'd known for four years that this moment was coming. His heart, he admitted later, did freeze up a little, but at the same time he couldn't help but feel her excitement.

'No, Amelia,' he said. 'I wouldn't.'

Of course, George must have minded a little – any sane person would worry about their partner planning such a dangerous trip. Especially knowing that, in the years since Lindbergh's solo flight across the Atlantic in 1927, **no one else had managed it** – though many had died trying. In fact, including Amelia's own crossing, there had only ever been 17 successful flights, and they'd all been in planes with a crew. Now Amelia wanted to do the crossing **all by herself**.

I reckon there's a one-in-ten chance I'll make it.

pffft!

But, as ever, there were rivals snapping at her heels. Young Elinor Smith – who didn't think much of Amelia's flying skills – even had a plane ready. So Amelia's preparations had to be speedy and completely secret. Once again, she kept the important news from the rest of her family. She didn't want them to worry or leak the information.

The story that George put out, as her bright red Vega was rebuilt to carry more fuel, was that Amelia's plane was being prepared for a polar flight. The wings were strengthened and a new 500 horsepower Wasp engine was installed. The Vega was equipped with **the latest gizmos** too, including three types of compass and a revolutionary fuel system designed to balance the weight of the aircraft as the petrol was consumed.

A solo Atlantic flight would be **incredibly dangerous**. Of course there was a vast expanse of water that had to be crossed, and the violent, unpredictable weather; but the real difficulty was navigation. With no landmarks over the ocean, and no navigator beside her, just flying in the right direction was going to be a challenge. Amelia practised 'blind flying' – using only her instruments to find her way – until she was confident she could handle things without even looking outside the cockpit.

The Doubters

At a time when women were never paid the same as men for doing the same job, when they didn't have equal rights in marriage and property, and they weren't expected to do much more than clean the house and take care of the children, it wasn't surprising that people disapproved of

Clean my house, look after my children and make my tea. I'm off to fly my plane.

Amelia's adventure. But, disappointingly, some of her fiercest critics were women. Even women pilots doubted her.

One famous aviatrix, Lady Heath, wrote an article in a newspaper which hit the newsstands the day that Amelia took off:

WHY I BELIEVE WOMAN PILOTS CAN'T FLY THE ATLANTIC

Flying the Atlantic is plain suicide for any woman today . . . at least the first dozen will be drowned.

Of course, Amelia completely disagreed.

I was doing it for the fun of it. Proving to myself, and to anyone else interested, that a woman with adequate experience could do it.

A One-In-Ten Chance

On 20th May 1932, exactly five years after Lindbergh's successful crossing, Amelia was scheduled to begin her own attempt. The weather had been awful for two days, but a sudden break in the clouds surprised everyone. Amelia had to make a snap decision: **fly or stay**. She dashed home and got dressed in five minutes.

Getting ready is always the killer. You're too busy to worry when you're in the air.

Lucky elephant-toe bracelet

Amelia's take-off was once again to be from Newfoundland. Fellow pilot Bernt Balchen, who had been helping her to prepare, went through her route and the weather she might expect. Amelia listened calmly, only biting her lip a little to show her nerves.

Then she crawled into the cockpit of the big empty plane, started the engine and, with a few final checks and a nod of the head, **she was off**.

The first few hours went smoothly. She flew east with the setting sun behind her. George, waiting anxiously in New York, watched the red skies and worried.

As the moon rose, disaster struck. At 12,000 feet (3,650 metres) **Amelia's altimeter broke**. It was the first time during all her long hours in the air that this had ever happened. From now on, she had no way of knowing how high or how fast she was flying – which is a little bit important if you intend to fly using just your instruments.

A few hours later things got worse. An enormous dark cloud blocked out the moon. It loomed like a vast cliff, stretching as far as she could see, and it was much too high for her to climb over.

There was nothing for it. Amelia plunged into the roughest storm that she had ever encountered in the air. **She was flying completely blind**, and at night. She couldn't see out of her cockpit. She couldn't keep to her course. Thunder, lightning and howling winds buffeted the plane. A seam broke in the weld that held the new exhaust in place. Amelia stood up in her seat and peered out of the window. Flames from burning fuel flickered brightly in the crack that had opened up – and the engine had developed a worrying rattle.

But **it was too late to turn back** now. To get out of the storm she tried to climb above it. Soon she noticed a telltale film of slush on the windscreen: the plane was at such a high altitude it was icing up. But before Amelia had a chance to react, **the Vega suddenly started pinwheeling down**, locked in a deadly spin. Alone in the darkness, Amelia fought the tumbling plane.

Miraculously, she kept her cool. She knew her only hope was that the warmer air lower down would melt the ice in time for her to regain control. She allowed herself to fall. But with a broken altimeter she had no idea how low she was getting – and, much worse, how near she was to the sea.

Just in time, she spotted whitecaps frothing on the surface of the ocean. Using all her strength and skill she brought the plane level. **She had been seconds away from death**.

But she was not safe yet. Not knowing her height, she had to fly a delicate line between the surging sea below and the dangerous freezing conditions above. Whenever she tried to climb higher, her plane froze up again. So for the rest of the night she was forced to fly agonizingly close to the sea, constantly aware that **she was one slip away from the waiting water**.

It was a terrifying few hours – but Amelia's ordeal was far from over. As the sun rose and warmed the air, she was able to climb to a safer height. She knew that she should probably have been within sight of land by now, but the sea (and any land) was still invisible through the fog and clouds. She couldn't work out for certain where she was.

Worried that she would miss landfall, she descended towards the dangerous waves again. As she went down, she flicked on her reserve fuel tank, and discovered that the pipes were leaking. Petrol began dripping on her shoulder, and **flammable fumes filled the cabin**. She could see flames still flickering in the exhaust, the split appeared to be getting wider, and she worried that the plane was about to explode.

Amelia still kept her cool and decided to land as soon as she could. In fact, she was so worried that she wasn't going to make it that she wasted precious fuel circling a fishing boat.

Then she ran hard for the coast. The last few miles were agony, with fumes from the leaking fuel filling the plane and the flames still burning. **Every second could have been her last**.

Amelia's Eventful Atlantic Crossing

Finally, gloriously, Amelia was flying over the green fields of Teelin Head, County Donegal, Ireland, searching for a place flat enough to land.

I did not kill a cow in landing – unless one died of fright. The horses, sheep and cows in Londonderry were not used to airplanes, and so, as I flew low, they jumped up and down and displayed certain disquiet. Consequently I selected the best pasture I could find and settled down in it.

An astonished farmhand named Danny McCallion was standing in the field and watched as the cherry-red plane bumped to a stop just by him. He was even more astonished when **the most famous woman in the world** leaned out of the cockpit and asked:

Where am I?

Err, Gallagher's pasture . . .

Where's that?!

Amelia was exhausted, relieved and frustrated and she didn't know exactly where she was but she knew she'd made it; **she'd flown right the way across the Atlantic**.

8   AMELIA SOARS EVEN HIGHER

Amelia had done something spectacular, and in doing it she obliterated every record going.

✈ She'd flown 2,026 miles (3,260 kilometres) in 14 hours and 54 minutes SOLO, breaking the previous record of 16 hours and 12 minutes set by a team of pilots (and smashing Lindbergh's time for good measure!)

✈ She was the second person ever to solo the Atlantic.

✈ AND she was the first woman to do it.

✈ She was the first human being to fly it twice.

✈ She'd also flown further than any woman in history.

But what really mattered to Amelia was that she'd finally silenced the voice inside her head that had been nagging at her for so long. **She wasn't a sack of potatoes any more**. She deserved all the acclaim, the praise, the prizes. Amelia – and Amelia alone – had done something truly brilliant.

What's more, while proving herself as a pilot, she'd discovered something else. **She was actually fantastic at long-distance flying**. She hadn't got tired on the long, arduous flight. She'd kept her head through all sorts of trouble. She had the endurance and the willpower to go much, much further. If George had hoped that this trip had got all the adventuring out of her blood, he couldn't have been more wrong.

Amelia wanted more.

Once again, everyone went bananas – and this time Amelia could really enjoy it; she was proud of what she'd achieved. She was cheered across London and danced with the Prince of Wales. With George at her side she toured Europe. Soon she had so many medals that she couldn't fit them on her chest.

Meanwhile, the world was still in the grip of the Great Depression – in America, banks were failing, farmers' fields had turned to dust and desperate hordes wandered jobless and homeless across the country. So, when Amelia returned, she asked that the celebrations be kept low-key. But her countrymen were having none of it: a bit of good news was exactly what the doctor ordered, and once again thousands of ecstatic **New Yorkers roared her through the streets** in a huge ticker-tape parade. Other cities followed suit. She was voted Outstanding American Woman of the Year in 1932.

But not everyone was impressed. The *New York Post* wrote: 'We think it an almost entirely silly and useless performance', and C. G. Grey, the pompous editor of the *Aeroplane* magazine, was even crankier: 'We cannot think why she did it, except of course for her own gratification. It does nothing for the good of aviation.'

It is safe to say that C. G. Grey got this spectacularly wrong. It was precisely because Amelia had gone just 'for the fun of it' that her flight was so important. She'd shown that women had just as much of a right to go on crazy, amazing, dangerous adventures as men. No matter what C. G. Grey thought, **modern women didn't have to stay at home**, stay quiet or stay in their place.

Girl Power

As well as giving courage to millions of women and girls, Amelia tried to inspire them in other ways too.

Amelia's Passion for Fashion

Amelia had been a major fashion icon for years. Her relaxed, practical style – leather jackets, wool slacks and riding boots – were a constant inspiration not just to fashion designers but to everyday women too.

She even launched a fashion line for the modern woman, which was available in certain department stores. In fact, she was probably the first ever celebrity fashion designer!

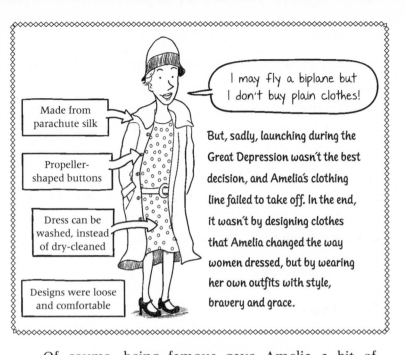

I may fly a biplane but I don't buy plain clothes!

Made from parachute silk

Propeller-shaped buttons

Dress can be washed, instead of dry-cleaned

Designs were loose and comfortable

But, sadly, launching during the Great Depression wasn't the best decision, and Amelia's clothing line failed to take off. In the end, it wasn't by designing clothes that Amelia changed the way women dressed, but by wearing her own outfits with style, bravery and grace.

Of course, being famous gave Amelia a bit of power as well. Politicians at the time were generally disliked because of America's desperate situation, and many begged Amelia to visit, hoping a little dusting of her popularity might rub off on them. President Hoover invited her to the White House – but it wasn't enough to save him in the elections. After Franklin D. Roosevelt became president and took over in the White House, in 1933, he had her over all the time. She had something in common with Eleanor Roosevelt, the new first lady: both of them supported women's rights. **They soon became firm friends**.

Gossips in Washington buzzed with the news that a slim, quiet woman in a white dress had taken

Mrs Roosevelt on a flight over the city to see the sights. She'd piloted the big transport plane without even removing her long, white kid gloves.

Er . . . maybe it's time to straighten her up now, Eleanor?

It wasn't hard to guess who the gossips were whispering about.

Flying Costs A Packet

Amelia could never be accused of taking it easy. With George's help she continued to slog across the country on gruelling lecture tours, spreading her message not only to the powerful, but to the masses as well. Over the next few years she averaged about **140 speeches a year**. This got her a lot of money for fuel. A week's worth of speaking engagements could bring in as much as $2,400 – that's about £35,043 in today's money!

Amelia would have been rich if she hadn't spent it all on flying. Especially now her plans were getting bigger and more expensive. She set her sights on a new plane, sold her beloved 'little red bus' to the National Air and Space Museum in Washington – where you can still see it today – and bought the latest Vega to take its place.

Vega Hi-Speed Special

She's got a cantilever one-piece wing and a spruce veneer monocoque fuselage for great overall strength and reduced weight, and the tail surfaces have all been improved.

I'll take her!

Speed: 200 mph (320km/h)

FOR SALE

Meanwhile, George's career had taken him out to California to work in the movies. He and Amelia bought a house high in the Hollywood hills. Through the window, **the vast Pacific Ocean glittered invitingly**.

And so, at Christmas in 1934, Amelia, George and the new plane sailed for Hawaii. She wanted to fly solo from those far-off islands back to the mainland. It was yet another deadly flight.

There were the usual grumblings. **Ten pilots had already died** trying to make the trip. And only a month before, a military plane had disappeared on the same route, resulting in an enormous search-and-rescue operation. Miserable old C. G. Grey, writing in the *Aeroplane*, was not impressed. He called the flight 'a useless adventure'. Amelia was 36 years old, he said, and ought to know better.

Honestly! The greatest hazard I had to overcome was the criticism for even attempting the flight.

Even her sponsors in Hawaii tried to make her pull out, but Amelia was right to feel confident: she'd already proved her chops as a pilot. And now she was carrying the latest radio equipment – which would not only help her steer but, even more miraculously, allow her to communicate with George and the rest of America while she was flying.

After a tricky take-off, weighed down as usual by the huge load of fuel, **Amelia's flight went like a dream**. The new Vega flew perfectly. Amateur radio enthusiasts tuned in to hear her calm voice reporting every quarter of an hour that everything was OK.

Stars outside my cockpit window look near enough to touch.

Radio stations relayed Amelia's broadcasts to their listeners. All across America, ordinary **Americans waited by their radio sets in their pyjamas**, tuning in to live updates of the flight. This was a new kind of news – and it gave Amelia a new kind of celebrity. They didn't care what grumpy old men were saying in newspapers. People felt like they were flying along with her, living her adventures, and they loved her even more.

When Amelia announced over the radio that she would soon be landing in San Francisco, thousands of people rushed to greet her. Around 10,000 of them waited at the airfield in pouring rain and cheered her from the plane.

Are you ready to stop flying now, Amelia?

Not while there's life in this old horse, buddy.

It was the first solo flight from Hawaii to the American mainland by anyone, man or woman. Hardly able to contain his enthusiasm, President Roosevelt said:

> *You have scored again . . . [and] shown even the doubting Thomases that aviation is a science which cannot be limited to men only.*

Hóla Mexico

But Amelia was not done yet. Her next adventure, three months later, in April 1935, was to be another first. The plan was to fly from Los Angeles to Mexico City, and from there to New York – a trip of nearly 4,000 miles (6,437 kilometres), far longer than her Atlantic flight had been. The section over the Gulf of Mexico was considered particularly dangerous, and once again **many people urged her not to try**, including her friend Wiley Post – himself a great record-breaking airman.

Amelia, don't do it. It's too dangerous.

Wiley Post – first man to fly solo around the world

Pah! I can't wait to get going!

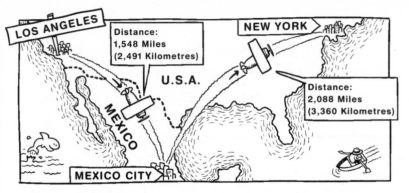

Amelia was right to be confident, because **she was flying like an angel**. She hardly strayed off track. Even when a failing fuel pump had meant she had to put down a little early in yet another cactus desert. But the bumpy landing didn't put her off. After a triumphant arrival in Mexico City, and several banquets, she took off for New York at dawn.

She climbed to 10,000 feet (3,000 metres), skimming over the mountains that ringed the city. The majestic volcano Popocatepetl lifted its snowy head to the dawn as she carefully shepherded her fuel-laden plane over the mountains and out to sea.

Of course no flight ever passed without some emergency. When she was far out over the Gulf, her engine overheated. Amelia didn't panic, she just turned it off – and flew for a short time without any power, like a glider. When she switched the engine back on, it was working again!

What if I switch it off and on again?

Her cool head had kept her safe, but right then and there she made a promise to herself that she'd never fly over a large body of water in a plane with just a single engine again – it was far too dangerous. She was obviously planning her next trip already – and it was likely to involve a whole lot of water.

Thousands of people had gathered to greet her as she landed in New York. They carried her out of the plane on their shoulders – everyone grabbing hold – and **Amelia surfed the crowd**! In fact the welcome was so intense that it was almost the end of her. A wedge of policemen had to rush in to prevent her from being pulled apart by her admirers.

Amelia's popularity was stratospheric. She was a giant, a megastar, a colossus.

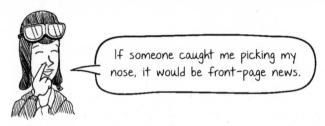

If someone caught me picking my nose, it would be front-page news.

Along with Adolf Hitler and Charlie Chaplin, in 1935 **she was one of the most recognized people in the world**. It wasn't always fun to be watched, so when Dr Edward C. Elliott, president of Purdue University in Indiana, offered Amelia a part-time teaching job, she jumped at the chance to take it easy.

Midnight Chats

Compared to the roar and rush of Amelia's usual life, campus life was blissfully quiet, and after years on the lecture circuit, giving talks to students hardly seemed like work at all. Better than that, Amelia discovered that she loved talking to her students. As ever she was easy and informal – sometimes she sat on the floor of the dorms, surrounded by girls, chatting all night. She'd been hired to inspire Purdue's female students to explore new careers, and she quickly began to do it in her own, unconventional way.

In her lectures at Purdue, Amelia didn't hide how radical her views had become – for the 1930s at least! She believed that women got a bad deal. **Education was everything** – but the current system was unfair.

All women's opportunities were limited by their sex, not what they could actually do.

A great many boys would be better off making pies, and a great many girls would be better off designing planes. Don't let the world push you around!

During their midnight chats Amelia went even further. She urged the girls to study whatever they wanted, not to get married right away, to be the person they wanted to be. **It was thrilling and radical** – and for many girls it was the first time that they'd heard anyone say anything like this. Her students loved her for it.

Dr Elliott recognized the effect Amelia was having and was keen to tie her even closer to the university. Over dinner one evening, he asked what her dreams were, and if there was anything Purdue could do to help her realize them.

Funnily enough, there was!

9   AMELIA FLIES THE WORLD

Amelia had always dreamed big. And there was one dream that was bigger than all the others. The ultimate escapade.

Imagine soaring above the deepest darkest jungles and the widest, most desolate deserts. Imagine conquering every ocean. Imagine waking up every morning in a city with a name plucked from the storybooks. **This would be the greatest adventure of all**. The trip to end all trips. No wonder Amelia couldn't stop thinking of it.

She wanted to fly around the world.

Amelia's friend Wiley Post had famously flown around the world twice, then died on another flight, in 1935. Like other pilots he'd used the easier, safer routes to the north, where the world was thinner, and the distance around it shorter, the winds were friendlier and the journey took much less time.

I wanted to do it properly and zip right around the World's waistline.

The tried-and-tested route

Amelia's daredevil route

Amelia's plan was to circle the Earth flying along the equator, **a distance of 29,000 miles** (46,670 kilometres). This was the fattest and longest path around the world, and the winds would be much less reliable. It was an awesome challenge. Amelia would be the first person to do it. She knew it would test her endurance and skill to the absolute limit.

The Big One

So when Dr Elliott asked Amelia if she had a dream, she was ready with her answer. She wanted help getting the funding together to buy a plane – and she was going to need a big one, filled with the latest equipment and a team of people to support her. She pitched the idea as a kind of flying laboratory – but everyone knew that, for Amelia, the adventure was much more important than the science, and they didn't mind.

There was no way that Amelia could fly this trip alone. Keeping on course and flying the plane by herself would be impossible. She would also need to refuel every day – and she'd be taking off from a different airport each morning. Many of the places she'd be landing in had **never seen a plane before**.

She needed a navigator and depots dotted around the world to supply and refuel the plane. The journey took a year just to plan and prepare. The plane alone cost $80,000 dollars (about £1.1 million in today's money). It was a Lockheed Electra – **much bigger than the old Vega**, so big in fact that just holding the stick steady took all her strength.

The plane arrived on 24th July 1936, Amelia's thirty-ninth birthday. It was outfitted with the latest radio equipment, including a trailing antenna that hung 250 feet (76 metres) below the plane and had to be wound up and down by hand.

Lockheed Electra

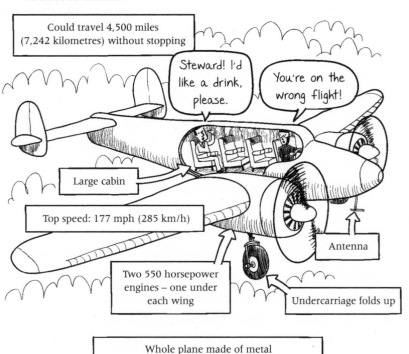

Could travel 4,500 miles (7,242 kilometres) without stopping

Steward! I'd like a drink, please.

You're on the wrong flight!

Large cabin

Top speed: 177 mph (285 km/h)

Antenna

Two 550 horsepower engines – one under each wing

Undercarriage folds up

Whole plane made of metal (Amelia's was red and silver); light and speedy

As the plane was being prepared, Amelia took flying lessons from Paul Mantz, a demon pilot himself and her technical adviser for the round-the-world trip. Soon she began to feel more confident in the larger plane, but when she took an exam on its new technology, **she barely passed**. This had Mantz worried, but there was no time left for studying.

The logistics of the trip were a nightmare, so it was lucky that Amelia was brilliant at charming help from wherever she could get it. She wrote to President and Mrs Roosevelt, and they got the navy on board. She was given top-secret government maps, charts and weather reports. She even got permission to use a new airfield that the navy was constructing on Howland Island, slap bang in the middle of the Pacific. This meant that she wouldn't have to refuel in mid-air when she crossed the Pacific, an extremely risky operation (who wants to mess about with long hoses and flammable liquids when you're miles up in the sky?).

Even so, **flying to Howland, would be the most dangerous leg of the trip** – even with several navy ships in the region to help her. The island was a bird-poo-slathered pimple of rock and sand, lost in the vastness of the Pacific. It would take an awesome bit of navigating just to find it. Luckily, Amelia had two brilliant navigators willing to work with her:

Captain Harry Manning, on loan from the US Navy

Frederick Noonan, a highly experienced navigator. He'd flown over the Pacific many times

The team were as ready as they could be.

Take-Off Trouble

On 17th March 1937 Amelia set out from San Francisco. She flew over the soon-to-be-famous Golden Gate Bridge (it wasn't quite finished). There was no great fanfare when she and her crew left. Bad weather had kept the team grounded for a month, and reporters had become rather fed up with the whole thing. The usual suspects had started writing mean things about Amelia in the papers.

The trip started well and the Electra was zippier than anyone had hoped. Even though Amelia was careful, flying well within the plane's capabilities, they broke the record for San Francisco to Honolulu by over an hour. After resting for a few days, Amelia prepared to take off for Howland.

There was no doubt she was nervous. It was a dangerous take-off: the plane was overloaded with fuel – and then there was a terrible expanse of blue water ahead. In the pre-dawn light, Amelia, Harry and Fred went through their preparations.

It was always beforehand that I got the jitters.

She set the Electra on the runway and opened up the throttle. The heavy plane lumbered forward. Just as they really started to accelerate, **Amelia made a bad mistake**. The right wing dipped suddenly, and as Amelia tried to straighten up, the plane swerved wildly to the left. All askew, they rode up on one wheel, the wheel collapsed and the plane skidded on its belly across the runway, sparks and flames shooting into the air.

SCREECH!

Spectators screamed. Inside the plane, even as they careered wildly off the runway, the crew kept cool. The moment Amelia knew she'd lost control she flicked the switches that connected the fuel to the engine – and **saved their three lives**.

The plane didn't explode in a ball of fire. Fred, Harry and Amelia were able to walk out of it unharmed. But when Amelia climbed out, **her face was ghost white** and her hair was damp with sweat.

Even as the ruined plane was being boxed up to be shipped back to America, Amelia was already telephoning George. She wanted to try again.

On the one hand, she didn't have much choice in the matter. The crash had been a financial disaster. **Amelia was flat broke**, and if she didn't make the trip now, she'd never have the chance again. Worse, after the crash in Honolulu, powerful people were calling for her to give up. Amelia was **criticized fiercely** – as was everyone else involved. If she gave up now, her reputation would be in tatters.

But none of that really mattered. Amelia didn't care about money, or what other people thought. She wanted to do this one last flight for herself. Her pride and determination made it **unthinkable** that she wouldn't go.

I was quite aware of the hazards. I wanted to do it, because I wanted to do it. Women must try to do things as men have tried. When they fail their failure must be but a challenge to others.

A Change Of Course

Amelia pulled in every favour she could to get the funds she needed, and the repairs to the Electra were completed in record time. Because they'd missed their window on Hawaii, it made more sense to **do the trip in reverse**, flying west to east. The weather would be better if they flew the other way around the world.

Barely two months after the crash in Hawaii, Amelia flew the Electra from California to Florida. On 29th May 1937, she announced to the world that she was going to try again and this time only Fred Noonan would fly with her.

She spent a last evening with George. It is hard in moments like these to know what to say to the people you love. Amelia seemed a little more troubled than usual. She said that evening that she thought her chances of making it were little better than fifty–fifty.

It's not a premonition. Just a feeling. I've got one more flight in my system. This trip around the world is it.

They took off at dawn on 1st June 1937.

Amelia's Round-the-World Scrapbook

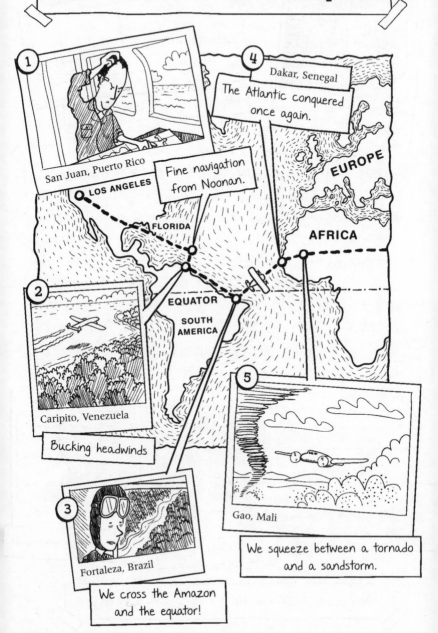

San Juan, Puerto Rico

Fine navigation from Noonan.

Dakar, Senegal

The Atlantic conquered once again.

LOS ANGELES

FLORIDA

EUROPE

AFRICA

EQUATOR

SOUTH AMERICA

Caripito, Venezuela

Bucking headwinds

Fortaleza, Brazil

We cross the Amazon and the equator!

Gao, Mali

We squeeze between a tornado and a sandstorm.

We've woken up at three or four o'clock every morning after only four hours' sleep and there have been extremes of heat like I've never experienced in my life. Utterly exhausted. Had to stop for six days' rest at Bandoeng in Java – had diarrhoea and terrible stomach cramps. Then off we went again!

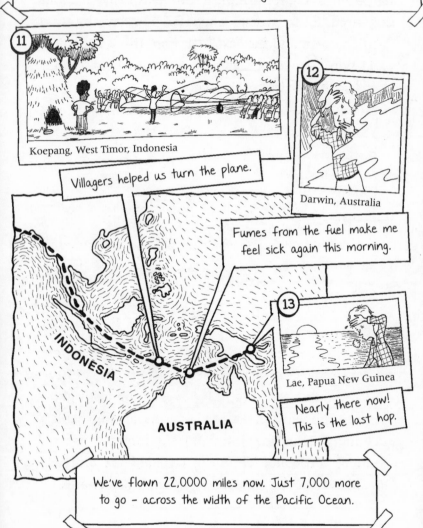

Koepang, West Timor, Indonesia

Villagers helped us turn the plane.

Darwin, Australia

Fumes from the fuel make me feel sick again this morning.

INDONESIA

Lae, Papua New Guinea

Nearly there now! This is the last hop.

AUSTRALIA

We've flown 22,0000 miles now. Just 7,000 more to go – across the width of the Pacific Ocean.

10   AMELIA'S FINAL FLIGHT

There was no doubt that Amelia was nervous. She had been flying for a month. She was belly sick and dog tired. Even worse, ahead of her lay the vast Pacific Ocean, and **the next little hop**, the 2,556 miles (4,113km) between Lae and tiny Howland Island, **would be the hardest** of the whole trip.

Howland was a measly 0.5 miles (0.8km) wide and 1.5 miles (2.4km) long. It was barely large enough for a runway. Aiming for it was a bit like throwing a dart from one end of a football pitch and trying to hit a fly through the eye at the other.

No one had ever landed there before. Very few had even sailed to such a lonely spot. So, on 2nd July 1937, Amelia needed to judge everything just right – weather and wind, of course, but especially the plane's fuel and weight. She threw out anything that wasn't essential, **including her lucky elephant-toe bracelet**. She and Fred even chucked away their parachutes.

Well, a parachute wouldn't be much use over the Pacific, would it?

Everything was ready. Amelia climbed up on the wing and gave a brave wave to the crowd, then dropped through the roof of the plane into the cockpit. At a flick of a switch, the engines roared into life, and they taxied forward. **Everyone held their breath**. The Electra was overloaded with fuel.

The runway at Lae was 1,000 feet (304 metres) long. It ended at an alarmingly steep cliff that dropped straight down to the sea. Waves crashed into jagged rocks. The wrecks of several planes that hadn't made it lay just beneath the water.

For this take-off, Amelia was going to need every ounce of her skill as a pilot.

She opened up the throttle and the Electra tugged forward, bumping across the grass. After 500 feet (150 metres), the plane was still moving sluggishly and **spectators began to fear the worst**.

Four hundred feet left, then 300. The runway was disappearing fast but **the plane still wasn't rising**. A flash of smoke puffed from an engine. The propeller stuttered.

Two hundred feet left, then 100. Amelia must have been pulling hard on the stick, because the Electra rose briefly into the air. But then it bumped back down to earth.

Just 50 feet left. At last the plane's nose began to lift. But even as it did, **Amelia ran out of runway**. The plane dropped out of view and plummeted like a stone towards the sea.

With the engines screaming, Amelia caught the dive at the last second. She curved up into the sky. People watching said they saw the Electra's wheels skim the waves like a swallow dipping into a pool.

It was 10 o'clock in the morning. The crowd waited and cheered as the tiny plane grew smaller and smaller. Finally it disappeared over the great blue.

But that glimpse right there was the last time anyone saw Amelia Earhart.

Problems From The Start

Of course Amelia and Fred had planned for the worst. They knew the danger they were facing and they had several different plans and fail-safes to deal with the tricky task of navigating their plane towards a tiny postage stamp of land across the great Pacific.

Navigation

Celestial navigation:
reading the position of the stars, Fred would be able to keep them bang on track.

Traditional navigation:
maps, a compass and the sun would help too, so he could make an educated guess about the island's position.

Radio: there were several navy ships along the flight path. By communicating with them by radio, Amelia would be able to get radio bearings. The US Coast Guard vessel, the *Itasca*, anchored near Howland Island, was going to be the most useful. If she could get a bearing on the ship, Amelia could use it like a homing beacon to bring her directly to the island.

The flight started well, but over the radio Amelia's voice sounded scratchy and distant. There were other problems as well. Some witnesses thought a radio antenna had been damaged on the bumpy take-off – they'd even left some radio equipment behind to save on weight. It was cloudy too, so trying to read the stars or the sea would have been difficult even for Fred.

They'd been flying for 14 hours by the time the *Itasca* picked up Amelia's voice, and for four or five of those hours they'd been trying to send their location to the ship but with no luck. Amelia's voice crackled over the radio. There was confusion between the ship and the plane about which frequencies to use. Amelia had agreed set times to transmit her position, but she wasn't sticking to her own plan.

Eighteen hours into the flight, Amelia and Fred reached the point where they thought Howland Island was supposed to be. But **they couldn't find it**. They flew from north to south, as planned, desperately looking for land, or a long trail of smoke from the ship.

It was about now that **the crew of the *Itasca* began to fear the worst**. They'd been trying to establish a good contact with Amelia all through the night. At last, at 7.42 a.m. (Howland Island time), Amelia's voice suddenly crackled loud and clear in the radio room:

KHAQQ was Amelia's call sign, and the sailors were delighted to hear it. They desperately tried to keep contact with the plane, but **Amelia didn't reply** to any of their messages.

Then, at 7.58 a.m., her voice echoed around the radio room again:

KHAQQ calling *Itasca*. We are circling, but cannot hear you.

To their intense relief, the radio operators managed to speak to her this time and started sending out a constant signal to help her get a fix on the ship's position and home in on the island. Amelia acknowledged that she could hear them.

KHAQQ calling *Itasca*. We received your signals but unable to get a bearing. Please take a bearing on us and answer.

Amelia then transmitted a series of dashes over the radio, but she didn't keep at it for long enough and **the ship couldn't get a bearing** on her plane.

Instead, they began to broadcast on every channel, desperately trying to reach Amelia again. The captain ordered the ship to fire its oil burners, which sent **a huge plume of black smoke** from its funnel.

And if they don't see that, there's no hope!

Cough!

Splutter!

The smoke trail rose high into the sky like a giant signpost. But the plane was still nowhere to be seen. Then, at 8.44 a.m. Amelia spoke once more:

KHAQQ to *Itasca*. We are on the line of position one- five-seven dash three-three-seven. We are running north and south.

It was Amelia's last transmission. **The *Itasca* never heard from her or the plane again**.

Realizing that she must have run out of fuel, the ship began a desperate search at once. But hope was slim. With heavy engines and empty fuel tanks, the plane would have landed nose down. Fred and Amelia would have had to scramble up the tail of the plane to reach the life rafts. Another Lockheed Electra forced to land on water sank after only eight minutes.

Over the next few weeks 66 aircraft, nine ships – including vessels from the British and Japanese navies – and **4,000 men** scoured the ocean. It was the largest rescue operation in history, and cost over four million dollars – an enormous sum of money! But they found no sign of Amelia or her plane.

Of course there were black-banner headlines all over the world. America's darling was dead and there was a vast, public outpouring of grief. George, utterly heartbroken, arranged a further, private mission to go out and search again, but it turned up nothing.

Many people just couldn't believe that Amelia was gone. For months, years even, her family, her friends and the greater public could not let go of the hope that somehow she'd escaped. It was **impossible to believe** that someone so alive could now be dead.

Over the years there have been countless rumours, supposed ghost radio transmissions and reported sightings of Amelia, but no real answers.

Three Crazy Theories

Though no trace of Amelia, Fred or the plane has been found, some very strange theories have been put forward to explain their disappearance:

✗ Amelia was actually a spy, sent by President Roosevelt to investigate the Marshall Islands. Captured by Japanese troops, she and Fred were either executed or imprisoned. BUT there's no good evidence to suggest that this is true.

✗ Amelia deliberately crashed into the sea in order to kill herself and escape fame. She did say that this was how she wanted to go, BUT it seems a bit odd that she'd do it deliberately. She'd been determined to make it around the world.

✗ Amelia flew on after her last radio transmission and managed to land near a remote island. She and Fred lived on there as a pair of twentieth-century Robinson Crusoes. Investigators have found improvised tools, a piece of Plexiglass the exact shape of an Electra window and a tub of freckle cream, that could have been Amelia's, on the remote, uninhabited island of Nikumaroro about 400 miles from Howland. BUT they were probably just washed there by the sea.

One good thing did come out of the hunt for Amelia and Fred: there are now much more accurate charts of remote parts of the Pacific.

In reality, the end was the probably the most obvious one: Amelia, lost but dauntless, flew on across the Pacific. No doubt she kept her calm, as she had in so many other dangerous situations before.

At a certain point, when the last drops of fuel ran out, the engines of the Lockheed would have stuttered and then given out completely. Their roar, which had surrounded Amelia and Noonan for over 18 hours, stopped and an eerie silence would have fallen.

Who knows how long Amelia and Fred ghosted over the waves. It is hard to imagine them giving up. But the Lockheed was heavy and the sea was rough that day.

They would have had time to say goodbye to each other – two heroes flying over the great blue ocean to their deaths. The truth is, **gravity always wins out in the end**. It had killed so many of the pilots Amelia had known. She understood better than anyone that everyone's luck eventually runs out.

This time she couldn't shoot through the horse's legs.

Epilogue

Amelia Earhart has never died, not really. She lives on in our memories: her cropped hair, her shy grin, her slender frame, her iron strength and courage. True heroes die young, and Amelia was as brave as they come. Her legacy lives and grows. She showed us that women need fear nothing. That they can try for anything they set their mind to. That their future, like the skies, is open and limitless.

But Amelia didn't just set out to inspire women: she did it for all of us. Amelia knew that adventures aren't just something you read about in storybooks. She believed that **anyone**, with the will to make it happen, **really can live their dream**.

Then Along Came Jerrie

It can't be true!

Jerrie Mock was just eleven years old when Amelia disappeared over the Pacific. She'd grown up listening to her heroine break records on the radio and she was **utterly devastated**.

But Jerrie followed the paths that Amelia had pioneered. She studied engineering (the only girl on her course), though she dropped out of college to get married, and learned to fly while her children were small.

One night, Jerrie told her husband that she was fed up of staying at home all day. She wanted to do something exciting.

'Maybe you should get in your plane and just fly around the world,' her husband suggested as a joke.

'All right,' said Jerrie. 'I will.'

When news broke that Jerrie was planning her record-breaking flight, she was quickly nicknamed 'the Flying Housewife'. She set off on 19th March 1964. Flying a similar route to her heroine Amelia, 29 days later Jerrie became the first woman to fly solo around the world.

It took nearly 30 years, but **Jerrie finished what Amelia had started**. How fitting that the record-breaker had been inspired by Amelia all those years ago.

The First Female Fliers

Amelia was just one of the brave women who took to the skies at the dawn of flight. Just like Amelia, these fearless aviatrixes had to overcome tremendous obstacles to achieve their dreams and make flying history. And there are many, many more!

Bessie Coleman, aka 'Queen Bess', born in 1892. Being black, no one in America would teach her to fly, so she went to aviation school in France! Bessie was a daredevil barnstormer and the first African-American woman to earn a pilot's licence. She died falling from the cockpit of her Jenny in 1926.

Harriet Quimby, aka 'America's first lady of the air', born in 1875. Harriet was the first woman to earn a pilot's licence in America. She was also the first woman to fly over the English Channel – but had the bad luck to do it the day the *Titanic* sank, in 1912. She died that same year, when she was thrown out of her plane at an air show.

Amy Johnson, born in 1903. Amy was a British aviatrix and the first woman ever to fly solo from England to Australia – a distance of around 11,000 miles (17,800 kilometres) – in 1930. She set many more records and flew with her pilot husband (who even proposed to her mid-air!). She died in 1941 serving as an officer in the British Royal Air Force during the Second World War, when her plane crashed over the sea.

But they didn't all die young...

Hélène Dutrieu, aka 'Girl Hawk', born in 1877. Despite crashing the first plane she flew, Hélène became the fourth woman in the world to get her pilot's licence, and Belgium's first female pilot. She broke many records and was the first female pilot to stay up in the air for over an hour. She was probably the first woman pilot to carry a passenger and fly a seaplane too. She died in 1961 at the ripe old age of 83.

Elinor Smith, aka 'the Flying Flapper', born in 1911. Elinor became the youngest licensed female pilot in 1928, aged just 16! She once flew, utterly illegally, beneath all four of the bridges that crossed New York's East River, and also won the best female pilot award in 1930, beating Amelia. She was still flying in 2001, aged 89.

Neta Snook, born in 1896. As well as being Amelia's first flying instructor, Neta was the first woman to run her own flying business. She stayed earthbound to raise a family, but took to the skies again in 1977. In 1981 she was thought to be the oldest woman pilot in the United States. She died in 1991, aged 95!

Index

> Use these pages for a quick reference!

TU 26/7/19

I hope you've had a crashing good read!